SHAKESPEARE'S
Comedies and Poems
A CRITICAL INTRODUCTION

SHAKESPEARE'S
Comedies and Poems
A Critical Introduction

H.H. ANNIAH GOWDA

ORIENTAL UNIVERSITY PRESS

Shakespeare's Comedies and Poems: A Critical Introduction

ISBN 0 7465 0024 6

ORIENTAL UNIVERSITY PRESS
2, Salisbury Mansions, St Ann's Road
London N15 3JP

PRINTED IN INDIA

FOREWORD

Professor H.H. Anniah Gowda, the Director of the Centre for Commonwealth Literature and Research and Head of the Post Graduate Department of English at the University of Mysore, and the editor of the well-regarded *The Literary Half Yearly*, has previously produced two wide-ranging volumes on poetic drama in English. In collaboration with Henry W. Wells he went on to give us *Shakespeare Turned East* (1976), and *Style and Structure in Shakespeare* (1979), the former exploring to good effect analogies between Shakespeare's last plays and the classical drama of India, the latter continuing the investigation by focussing on Shakespeare's tragedies and histories in relation to the Sanskrit drama. The authors had intended to conclude their labours with a third instalment, but Dr Wells's death at the age of eighty-three left this part of the task unaccomplished. Now Professor Gowda has completed the wide-ranging trilogy of volumes with *Shakespeare's Comedies and Poems*. He is that rare author who delivers more than his title promises, for, in the thirteen chapters of his book devoted to the poet's writings he takes up Shakespearian comedy from the early *Comedy of Errors* to *All's Well that Ends Well* in the dramatist's middle period; all this in addition to chapters on narrative poems and the Sonnets. Professor Gowda offers a particularly enlightening discussion of *As You Like It*, the Shakespearian comedy he most admires, considered along with King Sudraka's *Mrichakataka* (c. 400 A.D.), known to the English-speaking world as *The Little Clay Cart*. Complete assent between commentators is not to be expected among Shakespearian critics, but all readers of this book—as well as of Professor Gowda's previous writings—must admire, indeed be astonished by—his diligence and informed enthusiasm. For Westerners such as myself he opens new—and unexpected—doors; I shrewdly suspect that he will do the same for many Indian readers of the book with his remarks on Shakespeare. East and West meet in Professor Gowda's writing as he guides his audience familiarly through masterworks of two cultures. On his last page Professor Gowda quotes the Prologue to the melodramatic play *Malati and Madhava* by Bhavabhuti. "How little do they know who speak as with censure." the dramatist tells his public, "The entertainment is not for them. Possibly someone exists, or will exist, of similar tastes with myself, for time is boundless, and the world is wide." Professor Gowda addresses these essays to all those for whom—like himself—the world is similarly wide and time boundless.

UNIVERSITY OF MARYLAND (U.S.A.)

S. SCHOENBAUM

PREFACE

The following pages represent an approach to the appreciation of Shakespeare that differs somewhat from my earlier explorations, especially those co-authored with the late Professor Henry W. Wells of Columbia University. In *Shakespeare Turned East* (1976), which is a comparison of Shakespeare's last plays and some of the classical plays of India, we considered the relationship between the acted drama and the printed, the use of myth and recollection, melodramatic conventions and comic types, theatre arts and artifices, music and setting, especially as they are to be found in *The Winter's Tale*, *Pericles*, *Cymbeline* and *The Tempest* on the one hand and *Shakuntala*, *Nagananda*, and *Uttararamcharita* on the other. Then, in *Style and Structure in Shakespeare* (1979) we made a more detailed study of the relationship between Shakespeare's dramaturgy and that of the Sanskrit drama. Characters such as the *Vidhushaka* of the Sanskrit and Falstaff were compared; *Othello* is examined in the light of the *rasadhwani*, or Sanskrit theory of suggestion; *King Lear* is considered as a *sutra* (definition) of compassion; and *Antony and Cleopatra* is treated from the viewpoint of an Indian classical drama of love, *sringara*. Thus, dealing principally with the tragedies and histories, this work interprets selected plays largely in terms of their style and structure and the dialectical relationships among the characters, yet both action and language also receive critical and analytical attention.

We had planned to continue this collaboration and make a study of the early comedies and the poems of Shakespeare; however, Professor Wells's lamented death at age eighty-three left our projected third study unfulfilled.

Unlike my *The Revival of English Poetic Drama* (1972) and *Dramatic Poetry from Mediaeval to Modern Times* (1973), which are intended for academic specialists, the present series of studies of the early comedies and the narrative poems and Sonnets is intended for the general reader, the student beginning his study of Shakespeare; as such, it is less a record of research and scholarly investigation than a collection of appreciations that indicate approaches to Shakespeare's work which will reveal some of the joys and delights to be had from the study of the works and suggest, especially to students familiar with the classical theatre of India, some of the similarities in theme, character, plot, and approach of Western and Indian theatre.

The quotations from the plays are from the *Pelican Shakespeare*, one of the most widely used and accessible of the scholarly editions of the texts. And because of the nature of the book, footnotes have been kept to a minimum consistent with correct attribution.

Though writing about Shakespeare is always a delight, reading him is an incomparably greater one. As J.L. Calderwood wrote in his perceptive study of *A Midsummer Night's Dream* almost twenty years ago, Shakespeare offers us "a major kind of knowledge...the inner forms and impulses of the human mind itself". It is hoped that the reader will be aided by the chapters that follow in his reading and appreciation of the early comedies and the narrative poems and Sonnets so that he may grasp the richness that Calderwood identified so succinctly.

H.H.A.G.

CONTENTS

1

COMEDY

The poetry and drama of the Orient (no less than those of the West) are to a large degree occupied with the theme of love; most of the classical plays of India, for example, deal with love and its many aspects. But while many sentiments and expositions on the subject are alike in the literatures of the Orient and the Occident, there are obviously significant differences of outlook on the theme even within national literatures. Place and time assure radically different approaches; in each of the areas, works of very divergent character appear. Accordingly, it is illuminating to examine and contrast some of the classical plays of India with the comedies of Shakespeare, for at the one time they elucidate their common themes and even assist in clarifying the nature and scope of each literature. Moreover, without any special consideration of the plays as representation, a single subject remains in force of thought throughout with contrasting variations that prove revealing. Each play is in itself a masterpiece of art and of emotional insight deserving the closest scrutiny.

As in Shakespeare, there is a tendency in the classical plays of India to transform tragic situations into comedy. Comedy and tragedy often encompass situations alien to their genres, but ultimately their original modes predominate. The likeness between the two theatres defines the essentials of all good drama; the differences describe outstanding distinctions between East and West and so delineate the peculiarities of each. Gone are the days when, to Englishmen, Kalidasa was "the Indian Shakespeare" and, to Indians, Shakespeare was "the English Kalidasa"—terms that were not critical but are gestures of international courtesy that suggested a full appreciation of cultural importance.

Comedy (Indian, Classical or English) is a rare creation,

and as art it is as valuable as tragedy; it has always challenged the skills and abilities of the greatest of the acting profession. Comedy offers a commentary on the age and, reasonably well-produced, it always attracts a sizable audience in the professional theatre. It holds a mirror to the civilization of which it is a product; it offers often very shrewd observations and perceptions in its treament of all manner of themes, including politics, religion, society, psychology, and art. But fundamentally, a comedy is meant to provide pleasure, not violent purgation, as is achieved by Greek tragedy.

There is little doubt that the comedies of Shakespeare are among the best examples of the comic mode in English; in the minds of many creditable critics, *As You Like It* is perhaps the best of Shakespeare's comedies. In India, King Sudraka's *Mrichakataka* (about 400 A.D.), also known as *The Little Clay Cart*, and Bhavabhuti's *Rama's Later History* are normally regarded as the supreme examples of the comic drama. A comparison of the English and Indian plays reveals some of the essential differences in method and theme.

The plays clearly are among the undisputed masterpieces of their respective literatures, and indeed they hold such a position in the dramatic or poetic literature of the world.

The two Sanskrit plays are apologias for pleasure, as Shakespeare's plays are for passion. Sanskrit plays, born of Indian idealism (like the comedies of the West) encompass satire, naturalism, and the particular seriousness and involvement with life that leads to the most communing character. Problems in life are plumbed deeply. But the Sanskrit playwrights, who shun tragedy, possess a profound conviction of evil and consequently a high intensity of moral earnestness.

Mrichakataka is a *prakarna*, an imaginary story in ten acts, written in poetry and full of sentiment, yet realistic. It is a world in which thieves, gamblers, political manipulators, courtesans, and housemaids play a great part. These ingredients alone bring it close to the characters of a Shakespearian comedy. Yet in content, Shakespeare's comedies are the more intensely emotional; the Indian ones are the more philosophical. As for their techniques, Shakespeare's are the more audacious; the Sanskrit the more elegant.

The Little Clay Cart and *As You Like It* are representative of the comments I am making. The two plays indicate the nature of comedy handled by the dramatists of the different civilizations. There are some common characteristics—almost all characters in Sanskrit and Shakespeare use both verse and prose. In Shakespeare, normally characters placed high in life use poetry; relatively little prose appears in Sanskrit plays. Indian playwrights eagerly seek contrast, and hence we have the admixture of prose and verse and of both naturalistic and the more stylized dialogue, each distinctly attractive. In Kalidasa and Sudraka most verse passages occur in the role of the hero, who speaks in a learned tongue, the chief feature of which is its lyrical and epigrammatic quality, which suggests a sky half-clear and half-ornamented with fine cumulus clouds. The open sky is the prose; the clouds, the formation of verse scattered across the smoother but less sensational surface of Sanskrit. The style is thus lyrical.

However, the two Sanskrit plays and the comedies of Shakespeare all suggest the diversity of the remarkable artistry in the plays. Its panorama on its whole extent is noble. The early, the middle, and the problem comedies have their own distinct value and appeal. They are homogeneous expressions of a highly sophisticated culture, and they reflect the life of the period. *The Little Clay Cart* reflects a well-developed urban, rustic, and political life, but in most Sanskrit plays the current of religious sentiment and folk culture runs strong. This may not hold true for the comedies of Shakespeare. They are not, as in the case of classical plays, divided into *prakarna* (not less than five, not more than ten acts); plot is not derived from legend, mythology, or history but from worldly life. However, it is the purpose of comedy to give pleasure combined with didacticism in accordance with Renaissance theory and practice. All Elizabethan critics assumed that both tragedy and comedy should teach, mingle moral instruction with delight; and Shakespeare (who derived his theories of comedy largely from Plautus and Terence) is more or less didactic in outlook. But Plautus and Terence were not universally respected : Roger Ascham considered that in Plautus and Terence there is "base stuffe for that scholar, that should becum hereafter, either a good minister in Religion, or a Civil Gentleman in service of his Prince and Country".[1] Ascham's statement was made in a reply to Sir

Thomas Elyot, who considered that comedies were not "a doctrinal of rybaudrie" but rather "a picture, or as it were, a mirror of man's life, wherein iuell is nat taught but discovered; to the intent that men beholdynge the promptness of youth unto voice, the snares of harlots and baudes laide for young myndes, the diseeipts of seruantes, the chaunces of fortune contrary to mennes expectation, they being thereof warned may prepare themself to resist or preuente occassion."[2]

Many Elizabethan critics who wrote on the theatre were replying to attacks by Gosson and others; they could not, and would not, wish to defend comedy on the ground that it provided a temporary release from the shackles of morality. They felt unconstrained to say that good drama was essentially didactic. Plays, averred Nashem, were "sower pils of reprehension wrapt up in sweete words"; and comedy, said Sidney,

> is an imitation of the common errors of our life, which he (the poet) representeth in the most ridiculous and scornfull sort that may be; so as it is impossible that any beholder can be content to be such a one.[3]

Jonson, too, declared that the purpose of comedy, like that of tragedy, was to delight and teach; but *Everyman out of his Humour* speaks of correcting the manners and morals of the age, and he had proposed "to sport with follies, not with crimes". Jonson always made derogatory remarks about laughter, but in his plays he is less austere. Many of his characters arouse laughter. He was writing a "comical satire" at a time when there was little cause for spontaneous laughter, and often he was going against the grain. Both frolicsomeness and didacticism are seen in Sudraka's *The Little Clay Cart* and the early comedies of Shakespeare.

The main theme of *The Little Clay Cart* is the love of a noble Brahmin for a courtesan; the play, like Shakespeare's comedies, has poetry, sentiment, realism, and politics. The wicked are converted into good. It is a synthetic work, a story of city life and manners with political features and a strong, persistent current of humour. Comedy, especially Shakespeare's, is didactic in outlook. It was meant to mingle moral instruction with delight in the work of the playwright. The comic art is bewilderingly rich in its techniques, situations, and characters. In classical India, too, it was the most enchanting form.

But in both comedy and tragedy the poets and artists penetrate the depth of human nature. Since the Greek plays in the fifth century B.C., the playwright has had to act as artist. The design of the classical and Elizabethan comedies was to lead the public into a way of virtue. However, comedy, by its very nature, is a much more ephemeral thing and much closely bound to its own day and age than tragedy, and it normally follows the language of the day. The pleasure of comedy lives longer than the pain of tragedy; yet the comic world is not an escapist, glamorous world but a very serious world full of problems.

Though Shakespeare borrowed from Plautus and Terence, the tenor of his plays is very different from that of his originals. Like the comedies of the classical times, they are written with a purpose, but they are wrapped up in a bit of romance. Not that Shakespeare is falling between the two stools of the classical comedy and the romantic farce, for he gives the borrowed material some sort of solidity. The Indian classical playwrights depended on the epics the *Ramayana* and the *Mahabharatha* and other stories of Buddhism and Jainism for their plots, characters, and themes, with the result that a classical comedy sometimes is loaded with philosophical doctrines. Sometimes, too, it is a weak evasion of reality, as in *Mrichakataka*. But Shakespeare takes great care to balance the religious and the secular. In him the religious outlook of the East and the secular outlook of the West seem to co-exist. The age of Shakespeare witnessed the birth of a new spirit in every sphere of human activity, and this new spirit, known as the Renaissance expressed itself in its rich variety in the plays of Shakespeare and his contemporaries. Comedies that are as serious as tragedies in their theme embody the new view of man and woman.

Sanskrit plays express the values of life with extraordinary eloquence and force. Both Shakespeare and the Indian classical playwrights are deeply engrossed with the meaning of human experience. Man and woman are studied with supreme artistic innovation. On the whole, the women in the early plays of

Shakespeare are intelligent, lively, and vivid—as are Shakuntala or Urvaci or the dazzling Vasanthasena in Indian classical drama. They have a more approachable significance to the modern mind.

NOTES

1. Roger Ascham, *The Schoolmaster* (London, 1934) pp. 211-12.
2. *The Boke named the Gouernour* (London, 1907), p. 58.
3. Sir Philip Sidney, *Complete Works*. ed. P. Feuillerat (Cambridge : University Press, 1923) iii, p. 23.

2

THE COMEDY OF ERRORS

Shakespeare had read some Latin comedies at school, as they were part of the grammar school curriculum, and it is not surprising that one of his own earliest comedies, *The Comedy of Errors* (1594), was closely based on Plautus' *Menaechmi*, with one scene suggested by his *Amphitruo*. *The Comedy of Errors*, Shakespeare's shortest play, is frequently padded out with additional material but has a brilliantly sophisticated structure. Its tragi-comic structure encompasses farce, comedy, and the tension and consolations of romance. The spirit is very different from his originals : Shakespeare is more ingenious, much more complex, and funnier, but he is also more didactic. Jonson had criticised Shakespeare's lack of naturalness in style and plot and had quoted Cicero's model definition of comedy, *Imitatic Vitae*, *Inago Vertitatis*, *Speculum consvetudinis* (that it should be lifelike, natural, and truthful). Shakespeare's reply came in the speech of Time in *The Winter's Tale*, and in the passage about grafting, in the discussion about the truthfulness of Autolycus's ballads, in which Shakespeare "mercilessly denied whose who insist on truth in literature", and in the statute-scene where the play's "questioning of Nature, Life and Truth climaxes"[1]. As in his other Plautine play, *The Two Gentlemen of Verona*, a fragile vessel, Shakespeare extracts two interrelated lessons from his material; the damage done to marriage by infidelity and the consequence of jealousy. However, it is exquisitely written in its lyrical and set pieces, though thin on plot, rudimentary in construction, and uncertain in tone. And the theme of mistaken identities was an old one—one that had always been popular with the playwright.

Act I, scene i of *The Comedy* is based entirely on Plautus's *Menaechmi*, but the spirit of Shakespeare's play is different. However, one can see the resemblance. *Menaechmi* begins with a Prologue that explains how a merchant of Syracuse once lost one of his twin sons (Menaechims, the citizen) in Epidamnum. He was adopted by a citizen of the town. Many years later, his brother (the Syracusan, Menaechims the Sozicles) comes to Epidamnum in search of him. At this point the play of confusion begins. The first act in Plautus shows Menaechims quarrelling with the wife, pursued by the parasite Pericules and arranging to have lunch with the courtesan Erotium. The first act of Shakespeare's play, although dependent on Plautus, is more serious. Egeon, who is under sentence of death, tells his story in austere lines; the opening speeches correspond to the prologue to *Menaechmi.* Egeon's state is lonely, pathetic, and he is sentenced to die by the evening.

> Yet this my comfort: when your words are done,
> My woes and likewise with the evening sun. (I,i, 26-27)

Shakespeare is more ingenious, funnier, and more didactic than his original. The whole play is based on mistaken identity and mistaken goods; the action is complex; the verse is rhetorical and vigorous, but it takes command of the thought of the many characters in the town "full of cozenage".

> As, nimble jugglers that deceive the eye,
> Dark-working sorcerers that change the mind,
> Soul-killing witches that deform the body. (I,ii,98-100)

"Come, come, Antipholus, we dine too late" seems to sum up the play devoted to eating and enjoyment. However, Shakespeare (using the basic plot) multiplied the twins and the possibilities of error in his play by creating the Dromios, and changed the emphasis of the Plautine plot. Shakespeare stressed matching courtship rather than the husband's relation with a courtesan, a theme dear to him. There is also reference to sorcery and witchcraft not found in the original; also, the play is set against a Christian background. Adriana, wife of Antipholus of Ephesus, who has an important status, has a confidante in her sister Luciana.

There are many more changes : the parasite and the wife's father are not used; the courtesan's maid and cook are transferred to the wife and changed into Adrian's servant and Nell, the unseen kitchen wench. But they are transformed into one figure towards the end of the play. Dromio of Syracuse tells his master, Antipholus, how Luce, the kitchenmaid wife to Dromio of Ephesus, has claimed him as her husband, and a list of her qualities then follows. The Dromio-Antipholus dialogue (III,ii, 90-144), which corresponds to the Launce-Speed dialogue in *The Two Gentlemen* (III,i), introduces a series of geographical analogues. The setting of *The Comedy of Errors* is shifted from Epidamnum, the scene of *Menaechmi* to Ephesus, which has echoes of St. Paul's Epistle's exhortations on the relations of husband and wife and master and servant documented in the play.

Shakespeare has used references to witchcraft and deception in the Bible and in Plautus as interesting dramatic elements in *The Comedy of Errors.* Ephesus, used as the play's setting, was familiar to a London audience through the Bible and also as a seaport and as the home of the temple of Diana. Shakespeare, as usual, is indifferent to the geographical accuracy of Ephesus. In transferring the play's action to this city, Shakespeare had in mind the story of Apollonius of Tyre, which he may have got from the Veziah Wender in John Gower's *Confessio Amantis.*

Whatever may be the source of this play, mistaken identity is its motif. After the scene of confusion which ends in Egeon's despair, we move to scene ii, where we meet Antipholus, a merchant from Syracuse. The play about identical twins has a single vision, uniform texture, and a genuine comic life which depends on misunderstanding. Another merchant from Syracuse arrives in Ephesus and conceals his identity (this recurs in *Twelfth Night*, where the newly landed Sebastian goes off to view the city while Antonio waits at an inn for him). Dromio's speeches in scene ii continue the comic form. Antipholus's talk with Dromio about the money he gave him is significant :

O, sixpence that I had o'Wednesday last
To pay the saddler for my mistress' crupper ?

The saddler had it, sir; I kept it not. (I, ii, 55-57)

This is a city of cheaters. Adriana feasts the wrong Antipholus while her husband clamours outside for entrance (III, i).

This serves Shakespeare's purpose of creating a farcical world bordering on seriousness. Adriana and her sister Luciana talk about men and men's liberty. Adriana's question sets off the comic muse : "Why should their liberty than ours be more ?" and Luciana's answer is, "Because their business still lies out o'door".

Action moves quickly, preserving the unities of time and place, the entire action taking place within Ephesus and within the space of one day.

Shakespeare makes a deliberate endeavour to lessen the market place atmosphere of Plautus by mixing dramatic styles of prose and poetry and much of the comic life and the world of "the fairy land" of "goblins, devils and sprites" (II, ii, 190).

Act V, scene i is the final stage in a crescendo of violence created by the beating of Dromio and the fight with and binding of Antipholus of Ephesus, followed by the entry of Antipholus and Dromio of Syracuse with swords drawn. Comedy is about to yield place to tragedy. The scene is set for the resolution of all difficulties, which gives a new dimension to the play, and the playwright never tells us directly whether Adriana's jealousy has any real cause. Egeon's tale of the shipwreck; his consequent wretchedness; his appearance on the stage as a lonely, pathetic figure without money and friends and sentenced to die at the day's end, borders on tragedy. Egeon's position is not really intense, and the doom hangs; it is weird, and the suggestion of sorcery and witchcraft in Ephesus takes away the tragic intensity. Comedy runs parallel to weirdness and bewitchement. Luciana, when she pleads with Antipholus, seems to assume that he is to blame and tells the Abbess that he demanded "himself rough, rude, and wildly" (V, i, 88).

But Antipholus's wild behaviour, as far as we see it in the play, is to have dinner, duly chaperoned, with "a wench of excellent discourse,/Pretty and witty, wild and yet, too, gentle" (III, i, 109-110). He does this very well after he has been shut out of his own house. In a play where hilarious Doctor Pinch is described in such terms as "hungry", "leanfaced", "hallow-eyed", "a mere anatomy", and "a living dead man", the courtesan is remarkably mercenary: "Sir, I must have that diamond from you" (V, i, 391). It is worth forty ducats; she will be satisfied with no less.

Shakespeare's characters, although derived from Plautus, are very human. He humanises the Plautine manners and at the same time "stooped to truth and moralised" his theme.[2] However, a modern production of *The Comedy of Errors* at the Open Air Theatre, Regent's Park (June 1981) seemed to keep up the hilarious spirit.[3] Thus the play moves quickly through "concernment and a sense of friendly revelry",[4] as here and in *Love's Labour's Lost*. The Roman comedy of confusion, written with much economy and achieving a sense of distance through the multiplying of farcical events in the last scene, emphasises the joys of the family reunion. The playwright reduces the audience's involvement by the very speed with which incident follows incident. Coleridge saw the play as a farce, to be distinguished from comedy: "A proper farce is mainly distinguished from comedy by the license allowed, and even required in the fable in order to produce strange and laughable situations."[5]

However, Shakespeare is interested in emphasizing marriage and courtship. Early in the play Adriana complains to Luciana the speech addressed, as she thinks, to her erring husband :

Ay, ay, Antipholus, look strange and frown.
Some other mistress hath thy sweet aspects;
I am not Adriana, nor thy wife. (II, ii, 110-12)

Luciana advises Adriana on the duty of submission and of her speaking with Antipholus (the wrong one again) but more dramatically and emphatically in the final scene, when Adriana is convicted of nagging by her own confession to the Abbess, "She did betray me to my own reproof" (v,i, 90).

Shakespeare is ingenuous in reconstructing a Roman comedy into a neat structure as "the best plotted of Shakespeare's early comedies"[6]. He is deliberate in making the first and the last scenes serve the purpose of relaxing the mood of the audience with an appeal to sentiment and the remaining parts to be taken simply as laughable.

Comedy, weirdness, bewitchment, sorcery, and witchcraft in Ephesus make this play important in the early career of the playwright.

NOTES

1. Kenneth Muir, *The Times Higher Education Supplement*, 9 July 1983, p. 18.
2. Kenneth Muir, "Didacticism in Shakespearean Comedy", *Review of National Literatures*, Vol. III (November 1972) p. 47.
3. Richard Digby Day, having decided that Ephesus is situated in Italy peopled the production with every nationality, from German to, Irish, even using a line spoken by the Second Merchant after threateningly unsheathing his sword against Antipholus of Ephesus ("I am sorry now that I did draw on him") as an excuse for turning that character into a pistolpeace in "cowpoke" ("That Antipholes an't to funn Dang near shot him with mah gun"). (*Punch*, 10 June 1981, p. 936.)
4. Muir, "Didacticism", p. 47.
5. S.T. Coleridge, *Shakespearean Criticism*, ed. T.M. Raysor, 2 Vols. (London: Oxford University Press, 1930) p. 99.
6. T.M. Parrot, *Shakespearean Comedy* (New York: Oxford University Press, 1949), p. 105.

3

THE TWO GENTLEMEN OF VERONA

"*The Two Gentlemen of Verona* is not a great play: but it is a curious one, and a very wardrobe of 'effects' in which Shakespeare afterwords dressed himself to better advantage".[1] There is a considerable amount of truth in this statement, and Shakespeare is looking forward in *The Two Gentlemen of Verona* in that he is interested in introducing a double romantic story. He had always been interested in romance, the situation of the scorned lady following her sweet-heart appearing in his later play, *All's Well That Ends Well.*

The Two Gentlemen of Verona is an Italianate comedy, quite different from a *A Midsummer Night's Dream*, in which the effects of the dream world are set off against the real world and comedy arises out of the disharmony of the two worlds; but in the dramatic art of Shakespeare this play holds an important position: for the first time we get a glimpse of Shakesperean warmth in matters of health and sympathy with human relationships, even if there are no gentlemen at all.

The problem of love requires quite a different problem of artistry; love is set against a background of hatred and indifference. It is like the love of Shakunthala not being appreciated by Durvasa, a *rishi*, in Kalidasa's *Shakunthala*. Being in love is a very private state, and this state of mind dominates the lovers shown against indifference or hostility. Hence, as in *The Comedy of Errors* there is comedy stemming not from the situation of mistaken identity (as in the case of the Syracusans and the Ephesians) but credibility in understanding. There is mystery in the action of the play. Professor Cliford Leech has shown admirably that it is a wandering play, taking place in Milan, in Verona, and in Padua.[2] Compared to Shakespeare's other plays, it has the least number of characters and many more small scenes involving only two or three speakers.

However, the play has the familiar basic plots : the Valentine-Proteus-Silvia story (the faithless friend), the Proteus-Julia-Silvia story (the faithless lover), and the romance element, which remains separate. Although there are a number of inconsistencies (as is bound to be the case in an early comedy), the play can be seen as an experiment in Shakespeare's craft. It could be assumed that the play's scene is Verona, and it begins with Valentine, who has recently arrived from elsewhere and has fallen in love with Silvia, the daughter of the Duke. (He is not a sovereign prince, and hence he is informally introduced).

The two "Gentlemen", Valentine and Proteus, begin the play with a dialogue, as in Lyly's *Endimion*. The opening lines speak about a conflict of love and friendship: Valentine tells Proteus, "love is your master, for he masters you" (I,i, 39). Thus the theme of love and friendship is introduced. Valentine is in love with Silvia, while Proteus is in love with Julia. This is learnt from Proteus's long conversation with Speed, page to Valentine. Incidentally, there is a long but unnecessary interlude on Proteus's worry about his love-letter to Julia. His enquiry leads to Speed's reference to "Laced mutton", a term for a courtesan: "Ay Sir: I (a lost mutton) gave your letter to her (a laced mutton) and she (a laced mutton) gave me (a lost mutton) nothing for my labour" (I,i, 95-97). Thier punning is one of the characteristics of the early plays. Speed does not regard the lovers as special creatures; to him they are just strange, and not human. He does not bother about changes brought about by love; this is another common aspect of love. In this respect he is like Dromio of Syracuse. He tells Valentine, "And now you are metamorphosed with a mistress, that when I look on you, I can hardly think you my master" (II, i, 29-31).

The mixture of colloquial, solid prose and blank verse introduces variety. Besides, there is a clever balance of characters—Proteus balancing Valentine, Silvia, Julia, Launce, and Speed. Shakespeare seems to spend a great deal of time in describing transformations caused by love. When both lover and loved are involved, the love is "matamorphos'd" and the lady is even described as deformed "Ever since you loved her" (II, i, 62). This witty conversation adds to the comedy. The treatment of love is universal. Kalidasa's lovers behave in the same manner. The *Vidhushaka*, like a clown in Shakespeare, has the right to comment on the characters and the situations, and the comments become choric in character; the *Vidhushaka* shares the joys and sorrows of the situation with the audience. Here we have a similar situation :

Valentine : I have loved her ever since I saw her, and still I see her beautiful.

Speed : If you love her, you cannot see her (II, i, 63-65).

Speed anticipates Launce, the true clown, who is to appear in (II,iii). But the lovers are not allowed to live in peace; they are interrupted. Launce enters with his dog, Crab, and soliloquises: "I think Crab, my dog, be the sourest natured dog that lives : My mother weeping, my father wailing, my sister crying, our maid howling, our cat wringing her hands are all our house in great perplexity, yet did not this cruel hearted cur shed one tear" (II, iii, 4-9).

The news of Panthino that Proteus is "shipped, and thou art to post after with oars" (II, iii, 34), adds another comic touch to the play about love. Earlier, at the end of Act I, Panthino disturbed Proteus, the lover: "Sir Proteus, your father calls for you. He is in haste, therefore I pray you go" (I, iii, 87-89).

On the whole, the early love scenes deal with Shakespeare's favourite themes—insubstantiality and temporariness. Duke speaks of Proteus being worthy for "an empress' love" (II, iii, 70); Valentine says that "Love hath twenty pair of eyes" (II, iv, 89); Thurio says, "Love hath not an eye at all" (II, iv, 90); Valentine says, "Love can wink" (II, iv, 92); and Julia is described as "an earthly paragon" (II, iv, 141). Proteus's eloquent and demagogic speech admiring the foolish Thurio for winning the hand of a woman whom he himself intends to court is part of the self-deception that Shakespeare takes up more elaborately in *Twelfth Night*. But Thurio is happy when he succeeds with Julia, and it is clear that he will be banished. The joys and pains of love are ably demonstrated, and this seems a really lively treatise on love. As in most plays dealing with love in any civilization, declarations of love are made by betters. Valentine and Thurio fight for Silvia with "a fine volley of words . . . quickly shot off" (II, iv, 30). The clown and the lovers speak wittily, and they can dilate on love.

A Kalidasa would do it with the use of similes and metaphors in rich blank verse, while Shakespeare has the wit at the end of a rapier: the comic comments of Proteus, who is presented as a lover in the beginning, and Valentine as one unmoved by love. Julia loves Lucetta but does not want to spurn a man who shows her real love. But Valentine is dull, not quick enough to know that Silvia loves him; his lines are "quaintly writ". Act I closes with Proteus's concealment from the father that he is reading a letter from Julia. This parallels her lover's behaviour immediately before. Both Proteus and Julia love each other, and there does not seem to be any artificiality in their relationship.

The art of Julia's swooning has a parallel in Sanskrit drama; it provides a great emotional abandon and it is an established theatrical convention. In Sanskrit theatre, characters and scenes of the greatest emotional mobility are held together, so that the play achieves the spectacular aspect of drama and its gestures (in Kalidasa or in Bhavabhuti) are as requisite and powerful as in poetry. But the reasons for Julia's swooning may not have any philosophic background. In Sanskrit plays it would be related to mental occupation with the soul and its adventure, for the soul dominates many of the plays. The soul, by religious austerity, may become the over-soul or achieve complete *Nirvana*, for most Sanskrit drama, like the Greek drama, is religious in aim. The swoon that helps a soul to acquire *moksha* appears in *The Little Clay Cart*, where the hero, Charudatta, swoons when he hears that the stolen jewels, central to the plot, were left to him in trust. The heroine, Vasanthasena, and her maid, Madanika, similarly faint when the report of the robbery in Charudatta's house leads them to fear for his life. Like Julia, the admirable women also faint instinctively. The incidents help the dramatists to work towards the denouements. Later, Silvia argues that the painful elements (such as Launce's parting from his family) parallels Proteus's parting with Julia. Proteus comments, "Alas, the parting strikes poor lovers dumb!" (II, ii, 20).

The appearance of Launce, who seems to be a superfluous character with not much except to add to the comedy with Crab (a dog that possesses a name that speaks for itself), establishing a parallel with Proteus's parting and impending reunion with Julia and ends the second act ironically, with Julia planning to set out in disguise to find Proteus, whose fidelity she does not doubt. Her loss of love makes the audience know that her situation is poignant. She tells Lucetta :

He makes sweet music with th enamelled stones'
Giving a gentle kiss to every sedge. (II, vii, 28-29)

Shakespeare is out to document his values of love and friendship. He seems to be a little preposterous in the third act, when Proteus discloses Valentine's plan to steal away with the Duke's daughter. He wants him to promise to keep it secret, and the Duke acts as an amateur detective, becoming a forerunner of the spectator Duke in *Measure for Measure*. But he is not a very weighty character; he does not influence the action of the play at all.

In the Renaissance, friendship was considered more important than sexual love, the laws of friendship being immutable. Proteus's giving up Silvia is a gesture of friendship. Shakespeare has got himself into an artistic difficulty, and he wants to get over it. Duke pretends that he wants advice on how to pursue a love affair, and Valentine (who does not understand human nature) falls into the trap by recommending the use of a rope ladder concealed beneath a cloak. Duke is cleverer and trickier: "I pray there, let me feel thy cloak upon me" (III, i, 35). Duke insists on removing Valentine's own cloak, and he discovers not only the rope ladder that was to be used for the elopement but also the verse-letter addressed to Silvia, which begins, "My thoughts do harbor about with my Silvia nightly" (III, i, 141).

The Duke's behaviour is undignified; Valentine feels that in love-making he is still immature. But soon the Duke denounces him as "Phaeton—for thou art Merope's son" (III, i, 152). This image does not fit Valentine, who is unconnected with any mythological picture. Valentine, in his talk, appears declamatory; and when he is banished, he laments :

To die is to be banish'd from myself.
And Silvia is myself; banish'd from her

Is self-form self (III,i, 171-73).

He puts on the air of a braggart :

Except I be by Silvia in the night,
There is no music in the nightingale. (III, i, 178-79)

And on his banishment, he says,
"I fly not death, to fly his deadly doom" (III, i, 185).

But soon Proteus appears with Launce and offers him consolation :

Hope is a lover's staff ; walk hence with that
And manage it against despairing thoughts. (III, i, 246-47)

He offers him help, and Valentine readily accepts it. All this makes us feel that gentlemen are no gentlemen. When the gentlemen are away, Launce ponders his own love affair and deliberates with Speed on whether he should proceed with wooing. His love is a peculiar girl, but as he can never forget his Crab, his images are thus canine: "She hath more qualities than a water spaniel—which is much in a bare Christian" (III, i, 269-71).

His main cause of love is "Eve's legacy". The dialogue between the lover, Launce, and Speed adds to the comic elements of the play, and Launce takes delight in the discomfiture of Speed, "an unmannerly slave, that will thrust himself into secrets" (III, i, 369-70). This reflects the main scene—Valentine's overeasy confiding in his friend. More complications follow, especially Proteus's deceit of the Duke as Thurio has deceived Valentine. He speaks of "Orphans' lute strung with poet's sinews", but his quoting poetry is very odd. All this brings the episode of romantic love into ridicule, as the Duke's comment suggests : "Ay, much is the force of heaven bred poesy" (III, ii, 71).

After the scenes of romance, we move into the scenes of outlaws in the forest. The pattern of banishment is continued. The outlaws encounter the banished Valentine, "A man… cross'd with adversity", and they offer him the choice between death and kingship over them. They are frank in acknowledging their offences :

3 out : Know then, that some of us are gentlemen,
Such as the fury of ungoverned youth
Thrust from the company of awful men.
For practising to steal away a lady,
An heir, and near allied unto the Duke.

2 out : And I from Mentua, for a gentleman,
Who, in my mood, I stabb'd into the heart.
(IV, i, 45-51)

The faults of the outlaws are similar to those of Valentine. In this play of love and romances, fighting and eloping are on the increase; they are ordinary happenings. In the context of the outlaws and their situations, Valentine's love and his strange predicament do not matter much. Their reasons for choosing him as their king are intellectual and physical. As he is banished, he is close to them; he is beautiful and also somewhat of a linguist. When he agrees to become their king, he extracts a promise from them to do no outrage "On silly women or poor passengers" (IV,i, 72). The outlaws promise to abide by his condition, but their oath cannot be taken seriously, as it goes against their nature: hence these characters themselves cannot be taken seriously in the play; they are indeed lightweights like the Duke himself.

Soon we meet Julia in distress; she is in boy's clothes. Shakespeare is introducing the theme of disguise, which becomes pronounced in the later comedies, such as *Twelfth Night* and *As You Like It*. The play emphasises Julia's distress, which parallels that of Valentine. This is a very well-constructed scene that introduces the song, "Who is Silvia ? What is she, That all our swains commend her?"—probably sung by Proteus and musicians hired by him on behalf of Thurio.

Julia and the Host of the inn watch and listen unnoticed, and she learns of Proteus's business to Valentine, Thurio, and herself. The song strikes her very heartstrings. The quiet exchange between her and the Host is in prose, and it brings out the difference between the song and the blank verse of the other characters. The Julia we see here is no longer excited, but sad; her prose is austere and dignified, indeed meaningful, and it brings out her genuine quality, unlike the others affected. In order to emphasise this aspect of Julia, Shakespeare seems to have allowed Silvia to agree that Proteus should have her picture. When the Host falls asleep, the romance of sadness is highlighted. Later we see Silvia trying to escape with a highly romanticised portrait of Eglamour, which is in contrast to Julia's deflation of high romance.

The portrait of Eglamour strains our credibility, especially after the scene of deflation of high romance. Launce complains of the dog, which has made him suffer in spite of his love and devotion to it: this acts as a parallel to Julia's suffering because of Proteus's behaviour, and it is interesting that Shakespeare has established the Launce-Julia relationship so cogently. This also leads us not to take Silvia seriously when we hear of Crab's behaviour with her farthingale. She rejects the gift of Crab indignantly. Act IV ends whith Julia's anger, expressed in a dignified manner. She tells Silvia :

I should have scratch'd out young unseeing eyes
To make my master out of love with thee. (IV,iv, 202-203).

However, the baiting of Thurio by Proteus and Julia (V, ii) reduces the tension of the play. Proteus quips the old saying, "Black men are pearls, in beauteous ladies' eyes" (V,ii, 12).

Again the outlaws are on good behaviour with Silvia, but only Eglamour runs away. This brings us to Valentine, who remembers his love and asks the outlaws to accept his high code :

These are my mates, that make their wills their law,
Have some unhappy passenger in chase. (V, iv, 14-15)

Other tangles are resolved, and Proteus rescues Silvia but decides on rape; Silvia's behaviour is not very edifying, she says,

Had I been seized by a hungry lion,
I would have been a breakfast to the beast,
Rather than have false Proteus rescue me. (V,iv,33-35)

We sympathise with Proteus, but then we are shocked when Valentine intervenes and speaks of an "uncivil touch".

The play ends with the famous renunciation. The intention of the playwright is made clear: Valentine is made fun of as a lover; he is less discreet than Launce, helpless when he is excited, and didactic towards the outlaws. But he is interested in the friendship cult, and hence he is ready to hand over his love to the man who has just been trying to rape her.

In remembering the later scenes, one commentator points out that Julia's swoon is contrived; but it goes well with the practice in classical drama, and seems natural when the wrong ring is given. Proteus feels that friendship has been promoted and acknowledges Valentine as Silvia's betrothed. This turns the tables. Then he has to find employment for the outlaws, men "full of good/And fit for great employment". Valentine suggests a double wedding; Silvia, Proteus, and Julia are happy: "our day of marriage shall be yours:/One feast, one house, one mutual happiness" (V,iv, 170-71).

In this early play the comic light is distributed on Valentine, Silvia, Proteus, and Julia, but there also is the hint of Shakespeare getting interested in a double romantic story, which he seems to have developed as a writer of comedies.

NOTES

1. Sir Arthur Quiller-Couch, *Shakespeare's Workmanship* (Cambridge University Press, 1937), p. 60
2. *Vide* Introduction to *The Two Gentlemen of Verona*, Arden Shakespeare (London: Oxford University Press, 1954), XVII.

4

THE TAMING OF THE SHREW

The Comedy of Errors and *The Two Gentlemen of Verona* are good examples of the plays in which the comic tension arose from confrontation of characters and the style needed to suit these characters is not fully developed. Shakespeare, who had been described as an upstart crow, an actor who worked on others works and plagiarised, had created comedies whose comic element was in part a function of the style. In *The Taming of the Shrew* a sense of exuberant and uninhibited vitality and an imaginative invention is seen. Although sometimes it is crude and antifeminist, it is an interesting experiment.

As usual, Shakespeare takes up an old, inferior play, *A Pleasant Conceited History, Called The Taming of a Shrew*, which carried the detail on its 1594 quarto title page : "As it was sundry times acted by the Right honourable the Earle of Pembroke his seruants". Shakespeare, who begins the play with an Induction, keeps the drunken Christopher as old Sly's son, of Burton—heath. In racy prose he describes his origin: by birth a pedlar, by education a cardmaker, by transmutation a bearherd, and now by present profession a tinker" (Induction, ii, 18-19). Shakespeare expands the original Induction into two scenes. The Lord and his servants are given formal verse, but Sly slips into dignified prose as the Induction develops. He wakes up after a night in the forest with his servingman.

These fifteen years? By my fay, a goodly nap.
But did I never speak of all that time? (Ind. ii, 79—80)

His waking, dressing himself with fresh garments (attended by a new wife) and assuming a new identity is delightful, providing the comic muse a great chance to play its part. It seems a dazzling attempt on the part of young Shakespeare. Here is a character poised on the brink of some imagined joy with the old sense of "a Christmas gambol or a trumbling trick". But he is prepared to make the most of his immediate life:

> Come, madam, wife, sit by my side
> and let the world slip : we shall ne'er be younger.
> (Ind. ii. 139-40)

The new role sets off a chain reaction that runs throughout the play. The Induction, with Lord, Hostess, Page, Players, Huntsmen, and servants (and Sly as the central character) is a good prologue to a play that begins with Lucentio and Tranio talking about Padua and getting educated. Tranio wants to practise logic and rhetoric and learn music and poesy. Their conversation about equipping themselves is interrupted by the Bptista family, which introduces more dream-like qualities. Sly's head is in proportion to the ale he drinks. The boy who plays his wife improvises with a lively invention, and the tapster of *A Shrew* is turned into a shrewish Hostess. The Induction has a number of Warwickshire place names—Wincot and Burton—but the play is set in Italy, and the characters are close to the Mediterranean. Shakespeare elaborates the subplot of Bianca and her suitors, but where *A Shrew* has given two sisters to Kathrine, Shakespeare leaves her with only one. His subplot comes from Gascoigne's *Supposes* (1566). The theme of the pauper becoming rich is a common theme in Indian classical stories and in the *Arabian Nights*, and we have the story of a devotee of Lord Krishna becoming rich. Also it secured with Harmon Al Raschid, Philip the Good of Burgundy, and the Emperor Charles V. Talkative women being trained and a tinker being entertained had precedents in earlier literature.

In the Induction, Sly is the central character, and his waking provides a climax to the comedy—to the new life of the shrew. Katherine becomes subdued at the end of the play; her acceptance of a new role has correspondence with shrew's new role. Sly entertains the Lord when the pleasant comedy opens : "We shall ne'er be younger", rings true (Ind. ii. 145).

There are parallels: Lucentio enters a dream-like state at

the sight of Bianca; Petruchio works on Katherine even as the Lord works on Sly and Katherine gets a new identity.

Tranio and Lucentio meet the Baptista family. Baptista's worry is natural to any father: he is resolved, he says,

> ......not to bestow my youngest daughter.
> Before I have a husband for the elder. (I, i, 52-53).

But he takes care to introduce Katherine, the Shrew who becomes the central character in the play, and Bianca, who loves books and instruments, music and poetry. Lucentio, like Sly, goes into a dream-like state on seeing Bianca, of "mild behaviour and sobriety". Petruchio works on Katherine's mind even as the Lord works on Sly in the Induction and causes similar dislocation: the ultimate change in the shrew's character. Baptista has to provide

> Another dowry to another daughter,
> For she is changed, as she had never been. (V,ii. 119-20)

But there is a great deal of difference between the changes in the Induction and the play. Each change takes us close to reality, but Sly's new identity is false, while Katherine's is more permanent. Sly becomes a lord and watches the play along with the audience; his experience and transformation are important to the play. In his first dispute with the Hostess, Sly assumes his superiority: "Y' are a baggage, the Slys are no rogues. Look in the chronicles: we came in with Richard Conqueror" (Induction, i, 3-4). Initially, the bewildered tinker, Christopher Sly, whom the two servants want to deceive into believing that he is a lord, resists transformation; but ultimately he yields.[1] On his waking, Sly's question to his "wife" has echoes in the main play; the boy, who acts as Page-wife, says, "I am your wife in all obedience" (Ind. ii, 105).

In a way, Page's speech and the speech of the Lord about the life of Sly indicate the highlights of the play to come: they are an education about "the lustful bed", music, sport, and the taming of a shrew[2]. The comic scene, laid in the familiar Warwickshire country, shifts references to place-names in Italy—unlike in the anonymous *The Taming of The Shrew*, where the audience hear of the players' hustling preparation and their search for properties. Shakespeare tries to achieve this by the stiff blank verse which does not seem to last long. When Katherine melts to Petruchio, the stiffness of the blank verse is gone and some of the colloquial quality of the conversation of the Induction comes back. Shakespeare endeavours to make the audience acquainted with Padua; the information seems redundant, but it is worth a second reading. Lucentio opens his grandiloquent speech with these words:

> Tranio, since for the great desire I had
> To see fair Padua, nursery of arts,
> I am arrived for fruitful Lombardy,
> The pleasant garden of great Italy,
> And by my father's love and leave am armed,
> With his good will and thy good company,
> My trusty servant, well approved in all,
> Here let us breathe and haply institute
> A course of learning and ingenious studies.
> Pisa, renowned for grave citizens,
> Gave me my being and my father first,
> A merchant of great traffic through the world,
> Vincentio, come of the Bentivolii. (I,i, 1-13)[3]

When Sly speaks of Warwickshire, Lucentio speaks of exotic names—Padua, Italy—all to hold Shakespeare's characters in the plays to come. After the sensational prologue to Christopher Sly's Induction, which is no mere gimmick, we move to the play. Tranio approves of Lucentio's suggestions:

> I am in all affected as yourself,
> Glad that you thus continue your resolve
> To suck the sweets of sweet philosophy. (I,i, 26-28).

Padua itself was brutally money-conscious, and Baptista knows how to deal with the rival bids of Bianco's competing suitors. The playwright deftly weaves the Bianca plot with that of Petruchio, and one is in contrast to the other. The Bianca story is conventional in manner and temper. She takes delight in "music, instruments and poetry" and thus she is very close to the heroine of Gascoigne's *Supposes.* The story of rival wooers is common in both Western and the classical plays of India. Disguise is a common motif in most comedies; all lovers are dreamy; so is Lucentio, but not Petruchio. Shakespeare seems to continue the dreamy theme of *The Two Gentlemen of Verona*; the Master's dreamy posture is set off against the servant's realism, while Lucentio "burns pins" for the hand of Bianca. In a trance-like mood he says:

> I saw sweet beauty in her face,
> Such as the daughter of Agenor had,
> That made great Jove to humble him to her hand,
> When with his knees he kiss'd the Cretan strand. (I,i,164-7)

Tranio's advice is realistic: "If you love the maid/Bend thoughts and wit to achieve her" (I,i, 174-5). But Lucentio as a lover is very academic, scholarly, and only when he wins Bianca does he learn "the Art to Love".

The smooth love scenes between Bianca, famous for "beauteous modesty", and Lucentio are carefully composed and distanced from the audience. Tranio and Hortensio act as choric commentators; they comment on the fickleness of women in their disguise. Tranio, disguised as Lucentio, "makes a suitor to Bianca, gives a small packet of Greek and Latin books". Her courting is done according to the existing conventions; it is done romantically, while that of Katherine is done rather realistically, and even brutally. Bianca is in effect to be sold to the highest bidder, in accordance with the convention of the time. It is an orthodox way of arranging the marriage. In most cities—Padua, Ephesus, and Venice—of the early plays, money mattered most. Commerce is frequently used as imagery, and Baptista and Tranio, in discussing Katherine's match, talk in commercial imagery (merchant's part, commodity, etc.,). Gremio becomes the first suitor for the younger daughter. Baptista puts up the price; Gremio, Tranio, win. Gremio's kind is typical of the situation :

> your father were a fool
> To give thee all and in his waning age
> Set foot under thy table. Tut, a toy !

An old Italian fox is not so kind, my boy. (II,i, 402-405)

But Tranio (supposedly Lucentio) says,

Fathers, commonly
Do get their children; but in this case of wooing
A child shall get a sire if I fail not of my cunning
(II,i, 41-3)

The auction of Bianca is interesting in a world of romance where money is all-important: it is a feature of the early comedies, including *The Merchant of Venice*, But higher values are not lost sight of. Lucentio tells Hortensio, who wants leisure from lecture and music:

Preposterous ass, that never read so far
To know the cause why music was ordained!
Was it not to refresh the mind of man
After his studies or his usual pain ? (III, i, 9-12)

Katherine earlier says, "Her silence flouts me and I'll be revenged" (II, i, 29). She is cast in contrast to Bianca: she is determined, and loved by both Gremio and Hortensio. It is the case of two men in love with one woman. Tranio wishes to forswear his claim to Bianca in favour of Hostensio, who in turn says, "I firmly vow/Never to woo her more" (IV,ii, 28-29).
Both are envious of Lucentio. Hortensio, like Bassanio, hopes to be married to a wealthy widow, and Tranio to a lusty one. Marriage to wealthy women seems to be a common feature of the romantic comedies. Bianca becomes "a proud, disdainful haggard"—unlike her sister, who has to be tamed after marriage. But Bianca is more complex than her sister: she plays her part well in both love and business. She is romantically sweet, like the heroines of other comedies. Lucentio says,

The wisdom of your duty, fair Bianca,
Hath cost me a hundred crowns since suppertime.
(V, ii, 128-29)

The Bianca-Lucentio plot has the combination of sweetness and reality that would have interested Elizabethan audience and that pleases theatre-goer today.

The taming plot, which runs parallel, is deep and more psychological and educational in outlook. This is closer to the stories of classical drama in India. Katherine has to be disenchanted and made devoid of recrimination, and these ends are achieved. Katherine's role is tense and dynamic, and Petruchio's role as shrew-tamer is equally tense. Both hold the play together as a ferocious whole. As in Bianca's story, the motivations are also economic and mercantile; the relationships speak of lechery rather than companionable loving. The girls are to be educated; education seems to bother the playwright. Petruchio becomes an educator at "The taming-school". To Bianca's query whether there is such a place, Tranio says,

> Ay, mistress, and Petruchio is the master,
> That teacheth tricks eleven and twenty long
> To tame a shrew and charm her chattering tongue.
> (IV, ii, 56-58)

The education that the shrew gets is different from that of Bianca. Petruchio, who is determined to treat her with unrelenting cruelty, makes up his mind to "love her ten times more than e'er I did" (II, i, 161). He woos her with some spirit, and when she sings sweetly says that she frowns. He breaks her will to resist him. The scintillating conversation in which Katherine is treated roughly moves quickly to the climax in Act V. When Petruchio asks her to sit on line, Katherine says, "Asses are made to bear and so are you". Petruchio replies, "Women are made to bear, and so are you" (II, i, 200-01).
Katherine resists :

> To give my hand opposed against my heart
> Unto a mad-brain rudesby, full of spleen,
> Who loved in haste and means to wed at leisure.
> (III, ii, 9-11)

When he is not seen in good time, Katherine is not worried.

Petruchio and Lucentio derive from literary tradition and folktales, but Petruchio is more difficult to understand than Lucentio. He is exotic and speaks of his days gone by :

> Have I not in my time heard lions roar ?
> Have I not heard the sea, puffed up with winds,
> Rage like an angry boar chafed with sweat ? (I, i, 197-99)

He arrives late to the wedding, dressed "in unreverent robes", "in a new hat and an old jerkin; a pair of old breeches thrice turned; a pair of boots that have been candle-cases, one buckled, another laced", "and on a horse hipped with an old mothy saddle" (III, ii, 45-48). He is different from Lucentio; he is determined "to wive and thrive as best [he] may" (I,ii, 54). His visit to Padua is part of his seeing the world. Like the old scholars, he considers travel a part of his education, and he wants a rich wife. It does not matter how she is :

> Be she as foul as was Florentius' love,
> As old as Sibyl, and as curst and shrewd
> As Socrates' Xanthippe, or a worse,
> I come to wive it wealthily in Padua.
> If wealthily, then happily in Padua. (I, ii, 67-76)

Grumio describes his unusual behaviour at the wedding, how he drank wine, kissed the bride with "such a clamorous smack/ That at the parting all the church did echo" (III, ii, 173-79), and he characterises it as a "mad marriage". His behaviour at his own wedding must have amused the Elizabethan audience.

Katherine seems to be made for Petruchio: like him, she is blunt and unorthodox. She is cast in a different mould from Bianca, for she asserts her individuality and is not to be treated as part of Bianca's marriage arrangement. But Baptista tells Petruchio:

> Ay, when the special thing is well obtained,
> That is, her love, for that is all in all. (II, i, 128-29)

Bianca can be taken for granted, but not Katherine, who tells her husband, "He shall stay my leisure" (III, ii, 217). Her behaviour is of dramatic value. Petruchio knows how to deal with the shrew; he feels he owns her:

> She is my goods, my chattels; she is my house,
> My household stuff, my field, my barn,
> My horse, my ox, my ass, my anything. (III, ii, 226-28)

Petruchio's attitude is one of an owner of property. His wooing is far from charming; there is no passion or emotion involved. Act IV, scene i, which takes the audience to Petruchio's country house, adds much to the comedy of the play. Grumio says that his Master and Mistress fell "Out of their saddles into the dirt—and thereby hangs a tale" (IV, i,57). Katherine and Petruchio are also, as it were, made for each other: she is a match for him and she, too, is unorothodox. She does not submit herself to her husband as Bianca does, yet she is quickly made to yield; it is carefully worked out by the playwright:

> The more my wrong, the more his spite appears.
> What, did he marry me to famish me?
> Beggars that come into my father's door,
> Upon entreaty have a present alms;
> If not, elsewhere they meet with charity.
> But I, who never knew how to entreat
> Nor never needed that I should entreat,
> Am starved for meat, giddy for lack of sleep,
> With oaths kept waking and with brawling fed. (IV, iii, 6-10)

All this sounds crude and poor, even anti-feminist and thin. But Katherine is not of the class of Portia, Beatrice, Rosalind, or Viola—the pure, lyrical heroines.

Act IV brings about Katherine's discomfiture: Petruchio "kills her in her own humour" (IV, i, 167) and with kindness. All the picturesque culinary details given in IV, iii provide a knock-about comedy. Petruchio's treatment of Katherine is an exhibition, a non-romantic love affair intended to subdue her. It is unusual for anybody—more so for the citizens of Padua. More than Shakespeare's audience, modern ones may consider his treatment of Katherine in a bad taste. This is in keeping with the tenor of the earlier, cruder shrew plays, such as *Torn Taylor and his Wife*, where, when the shrew submits, it is either to "high, theological argument or to a taste of the stick". In Indian drama a shrew frequently submitted to the taste of the stick; however, the effect in Shakespeare is different: it does not seem to touch the inner self, and in this respect it is close to an Indian situation. "My falcon now is sharp and passing empty" suggests that Katherine is ready to yield, to submit. The taming of Katherine is a sport and is ably done. The ritual of torture and courtship comes off well. Katherine's obedience leads to more pleasant things: she identifies herself with her husband:

> Then God be blessed, it is the bless'd sun,
> But sun it is not when you say it is not,
> And the moon changes even as your mind. (IV, v, 19-21)

This is the exact position of a heroine in a classical story called "Chandi"; she is also converted gradually. It does not make for Katherine's losing her mind, but yielding to her husband; and as a subdued wife, she is able to see the beauty in Vincentio:

> Happy the parents of so fair a child,
> Happier the man whom favourable stars
> Allots thee for his lovely bedfellow. (IV, v, 38-40)

She finds pleasure in her new role as an obedient spouse, and the play's truly "a pleasant comedy" (Induction, ii, 130) which "bears a thousand harms and lengthens life". (ii, 136). The wedding banquet long remains in the mind of the audience, and the play achieves, in the end, "peace and quiet life" (V, i, 108) in Petruchio's marriage.

The play by the young Shakespeare comes fully into sight: it seems a dazzling achievement of the playwright's views on sport, play-acting, education, the taming of a shrew, and Lucentio's seeking a wife with a fortune. It has the warmth of fulfilled romantic love leading to sharing in marriage in a world of sharp actuality of the sort encountered in *Much Ado About Nothing*.

NOTES

1. G.R. Hibbard, in the Introduction to his New Penguin edition of *The Taming of the Shrew* (Harmondsworth, 1968, p. 9) sees the character as a number of cases of conditioning.
2. "In keeping with the tenor of the play, Michael Bogdanov's production began with a tall young man, unkempt and unshaven, loudly disputing with an embarrassed usherette who was trying to insist that he remove himself and his bottle of beer from the auditorium. She fetched an usher, and the intruder escaped them by climbing on to the stage, where he then went on a rampage, ripping down swag-curtains, toppling proscenium-arch scenery, and swearing at stage crew. In the chat that followed, lights flashed, battens were lowered and raised erratically, whistles blew, and one hysterical young woman in jeans, seemingly an assistant manager, was carried out screaming. When order was at last restored, the actual set to be used for *The Shrew* was visible under cold light; a complex of parallel flights of stairs with platforms on four levels. The wrecker of the scene turned out to be Johnatha Pryce, who played Sly and Petruchio."

   (E.A.M. Colmer, "Autumn Leaves on the Avon", *The Literary Half-Yearly*. XX, No. 1 (January 1979), 142-56.
3. In the 1977 production at Stratford, Lucentio and Tranio came to Padua on a gleaming Japanese motor bike.
4. In the production I saw, Petruchio, cracking a whip (which came down from John Philip Kemble in the last years of the eighteenth century) improvised on a line added by Garrick for his three-act farce *Katherine and Petruchio* (1754). Before Garrick revisions were so rare, as to have kept with Shakespeare : after Garrick came "additions to the orignial text", which cheerfully altered Shakespeare, slotted in a lot of Garrick, and added songs, see *The Times Literary Supplement*, 5 March 1982, p. 266.
5. M.C. Bradbrook, "Dramatic Role as Social Image: A Study of *The Taming of the Shrew*", *Shakespeare Survey*, 1958, p. 134.

5

LOVE'S LABOUR'S LOST

Love's Lobour's Lost is not one of Shakespeare's mature comedies, yet it presents certain difficulties. Hazlitt wrote, "If we were to part with any of the author's comedies, it should be this." Coleridge held the same opinion. Their judgments are still valid in many respects, except in the study of the style of the playwright. But somehow the play has survived in the theatre. It was first published in quarto in 1589 and carried the notation; "As it was presented before Her Highness this last Christmas. Newly corrected and augmented by W. Shakespeare". This shows that it was not a new play. In the same year a certain Robert Tofte, who (much against his will) was taken by his wife to see the play, stayed to the very end. During the course of the production he yawned, but later he wrote:

> Each actor played in cunning wise his part,
> But chiefly those entrapped in Cupid's snare;
> Yet all was feigned, 't was not from the heart,
> They seemed to grieve, but yet they fel no care:
> 'Twas I was that grief (indeed) did bear in best:
> The others did but make a show in jest.

The characters being "entrapped" in love seems a sound criticism, but the play had topical interest: Henry of Navarre had just brought the wars of religion to an end, and his love affairs were the talk of the towns on both sides of the Channel. The play suggests that his life of love (breaking his oath to forswear the sight of woman, if only for three years) was interesting on the stage. There are also comments on statecraft in the speeches of Dumaine, and it is suggested that Henry, who had been married to Margarite de Valois, daughter of Katherine de Medici, met him with a retinue of ladies-in-waiting at Nerac in 1578 after a long separation. This may have suggested the meeting of the Princess of France and ladies-in-waiting on her diplomatic mission.

Love's Labour's Lost, as recent scholarship has shown, belongs to the period of *Richard II*, *Romeo and Juliet*, the supernatural *A Midsummer Night's Dream*, and also the lyrical exuberance of essays in pure poetry, "Venus and Adonis", "Lucrece", and some of the early Sonnets dealing with love. It has all the features of early plays : the sparkle of wit and quick comicalities and the taunts composed for pairs of lovers. The playwright's mind is on the image of his dark lady, who is cast in the mould of Rosaline. Berowne is another character drawn in the round.

However, reference to the play is given in Francis Meres's *Palladis Tamia* (1598) and in Robert Tofte's *Alba* (also dated 1598). In *Palladis Tamia*, it is alluded to thus:

> Loves Labour Lost, I once did see a Play
> Ycleped so, so called to my paine.

It is one of the early comedies and has all the splendour of rhetoric: euphemistic statements and artificial diction with a number of allusions to ancient history and places. Unusually, no written source seems to have inspired Shakespeare, though he may have been inspired by the real King of Navarre receiving the embassies from France[2]. The King of Academe is also derived from history and probably, was constructed for a private courtly aduience. The stylised, lilting, and punning dialogue of *The Taming of The Shrew* seems to spill over into the play; the encounters between men and women are on a bigger scale.

The idea of Academe is set forth in the opening lines of King Ferdinand, and the idea of romantic love in a world full of suffering is soon developed. The King says:

> Let fame, that all hunt after in their lives,
> Live regist'red upon our brazen tombs
> And then grace us in the disgrace of death;
> When, spite of cormorant devouring Time,
> Th' endeavour of this present breath may buy
> That honour which shall bate his scythe's keen edge

And make us heirs of all eternity. (I,i,1-7)

So he plans to set up "a little academe still and contemplative in living art" (I,i,13-14). Berowne, Dumaine, and Longaville, his bookmen and his fellow-scholars, have to "subscribe to deep oaths" of three years' rigorous study and "Not to see ladies, study, fast, sleep." (I,i,48). Only Berowne is practical: he feels that the oaths are "barren tasks, too hard to keep" (I,i,48).

One with an Indian and ascetic background may disagree with Berowne. In our ancient *gurukulas* (the places of learning in India) the sight of a woman was not welcome. A student devoted to studies considered his mission a sort of penance and gave himself to it wholeheartedly. But the bookmen in *Love's Labour's Lost* do not seem to be unreal, although very soon they flout their oaths. The characters point out the artifice of their own behaviour. Berowne is different, as can be seen in these lines:

> A dangerous law against gentility !
> (*Reads*)
> " 'Item': If any man be seen to talk with a woman
> Within the term of three years, he shall endure such
> public shame as the rest of the court
> can possibly devise" (I,i,126-30)

He anticipates the arrrival of the French King's attractive daughter, the sight of whom will make the bookmen break their oaths (IV, iii), and who will hide to spy on their companions. It is a very witty and humorous scene in which they are all controlled by passion, which levels them all. It is "All hid, all hid—an old infant play" (IV,iii,73), according to Berowne, who makes a number of deflating remarks thoughout the play. The play's swift movement and humour are displayed in the opening lines, where Costard beautifully sums up the futility of their oath: "Such is the simplicity of man to hearken after the flesh" (I,i,210).

This is one aspect of the play; its satire bites deeper in its ridicule of Lyly and the University Wits, whose verbosity and fluid statements went against Shakespeare's grain. He was probably against the prose and the verse of the age, sparkling with true metaphor, image, simile, play upon words, conceits, and every type of verbal felicity. The use of Boyet as a go-between is part of the comedy. In the early and later scenes (and in the character of Holofernes, the pedant), Shakespeare is attacking the futility of euphuistic prose. Holofernes's description of the deer killed by the Princess as "sanguis, in blood; ripe as the pomewater, who now hangeth like a jewel in the ear of coelo, the sky, the welkin, the heaven" (IV,ii,3-5), is part of the attack on euphemism.

Nathaniel says, "Truly, master Holofernes, the epithets are sweetly varied, like a scholar at the least" (IV,ii,7-8). This is towards the end of the play and sometimes seems an unwanted insertion in a play entitled *Love's Labour's Lost*. The arrival of the Princess and her ladies; Boyet, her liaison officer and elder statesman and lords gives Shakespeare his natural style. The Princess's statement, "Beauty is sought by judgment of the eye", is sigificant; she immediately gets down to the business of tasking the tasker, Boyet, to know the pleasure of Navarre and whether they can enter "His forbidden gates". But their oaths are forgotten and the King and his men are ready to meet the Princess and her companions. The Princess and the King converse in the simple, fluent English of diplomatic business, but the King, after a business speech, speaks like a lover:

> But here without you shall be so received
> As you shall deem yourself lodged in my heart,
> Though so denied fair harbor in my house. (II,i,171-73)

But Berowne meets his dark lady in Rosaline, who recalls having met "a merrier man. Within the limit of becoming mirth" (II,i,66-67). His discourse is sweet and valuable. Their swift, witty conversation reminds one of Benedick and Beatrice in the style of *stickomythia*. In the light of this, we find the discussion of the French claim and the diplomatic business tedious. Berowne and Rosaline have exchanged wits: Dumaine and Longaville have exchanged eyes with Katherine and Maria. The scene of romance is continued. Armado employs Costard as his messenger with a letter to Jaquenetta, giving him remuneration for his pains. Costard is also a lover: his affections are transferred to a lady called Frances, and he goes on his errand cheerfully. Accidentally, he meets Berowne, which proves unlucky to him; Berowne gives him a letter to Rosaline (as the ladies will be in the park) and with it a shilling—much better than Armado's remuneration of a penny. Costard's joy knows no bounds; he makes a speech, explaining that Berowne had given him a guerdon of a shilling. Berowne is equally happy:

> And I, forsooth, in love !
> I, that have been love's whip,
> A very beadle to a humorous sigh. (III,i,162-64)

But he is about to become "a wimpled, whining, poor, blind, wayward boy". This is as if Shakespeare is shaping the character of Berowne; both the character and verse get into their stride and make an eloquent plea:

> A whitely wanton with a velvet brow,
> With the pitch balls stuck in her face for eyes. (III,i,185-86)

The whole passage is typical of Shakespeare's lovers: Benedick and Beatrice and Romeo and Juliet in their early scenes—or even with Rosaline when they danced together in Brabant. Berowne confesses love for all his fellows, who are aware of each other's private feelings, which are important for the make-up of the play; "By the Lord, this love is as mad as Ajax; it kills sheep, it kills me" (IV, iii,6); and somewhat later, "Like a demi-god here sit I in the sky" (IV,iii,76). He watches his companions break their oaths and fall in love. They are discovered *in flagrante delicto* of perjury. As one of "four wood cocks in a dish", he steps forth with hypocrisy; he has seen "a scene of fool'ry", "a King transformed to a gnat", "great Hercules whipping a jig", "profound Soloman to tune a jig", "Nestor play at push-pin with the boys", "Critic Timon laugh at idle toys!" (IV,iii,163-64).

"Moon-like men, men of inconstancy" feel that they are betrayed to Berowne's overview. Another glimpse of the chase of the Princess and her train with bows and arrows shooting the deer among the thickets of the park provides an interesting spectacle. The trick of the ladies works when the men return in their own persons: the ladies expose them. This exposure is in contrast to the early oath-taking scene of the bookmen. Berowne dominates the scene. The bookmen are doubly forsworn "again forsworn, in will and error" (V,ii, 471) for having declared love to the wrong partners, and Berowne speaks for all:

> Here stand I, lady; dart thy skill at me,
> Bruise me with scorn, confound one with a flout
> ... ...
> And I will wish thee never more to dance,
> Nor never more in Russian habit wait
> ... ...
> Nor woo in rime, like a blind harper's song.
> (V, ii, 397-401)

But Rosaline brings him back to his frame of mind : "Sans 'sans', I pray you" (V, ii, 417).

It is interesting to note that while the men are more serious about love-making, the women consider it as "bombast and as living to the time". This recalls Berowne's later use of imagery renouncing "Taffeta phrases, silken terms precise/Three-piled hyperboles" (V, ii, 406-7). As in *The Two Gentlemen of Verona*, the display of love is a matter of social convention and not a necessity. This seems to be the pattern of the early comedies : all is fair in love and war.

The scene of the masque of the Nine Worthies anticipates the Athenians in the play about Pyramus and Thisbe in *A Midsummer Night's Dream*; the playwright is aware that the response to the masque alternates between condescension and incivility; the audience is also rude. The whole scene is born of Shakespeare's knowledge of country theatricals, at which the behaviour seems to be common to all countries. There are the Costards everywhere who mispronounce and later get corrected, as Dumaine does here. When Costard announces himself as "Pompey surnamed the Big", Dumaine corrects him, "the Great". When the play is over, Princess thanks great Pompey, but Costard's reply is pertinent:

'Tis not so much worth; but I hope I was perfect. I made a little fault in Great. (V, ii, 554)

Sir Nathaniel, as Alexander the Great, is crude; he retires hurt; and again Costard makes amends:

There, an't shall please you, a foolish mild man; an honest man, look your and soon dashed. He is a marvellous good neighbour, faith, and a very good bowler; but for Alisander—alas, you see how 'tis a little o'er parted. (V, ii, 575-80)

The way the lovers fall from their early stand is carefully documented; Berowne's comments are choric in character. The scene of exposure is dramatically effective : the playwright takes care to remind the audience that the play is situated about the lower foothills of the Pyrenees :

Was that the King, that spurred his horse so hard
Against the steep uprisng of the hill ? (IV, i, 1-2)

The mishandling of the letter of the Princess to Jaquenetta by Costrad, an illiterate, is interesting, and the worldly exchanges between Rosaline and Boyet please the modern audience no less than the Elizabethan.

Thou canst not hit it, hit it, hit it,
Thou canst not hit it, my good man. (IV, i, 124-26)

In this exposure of hypocrisy, even Berowne does not emerge triumphant. He does not get a sympathetic hearing for his declarations any more than his companions do. However, before the play takes a serious turn, we have Armado and the pedants display their facility with words. It is in the words of Moth : "They have been at a great feast of languages and stolen the scraps" (V, i, 35). Holofernes's comment is alliterative :

The preyful princes pierсd and prick'd a pretty pleasing pricket;

Some say a sore, but not a sore till now made sore with
shooting. (IV,ii,53-54)

All this is part of *Love's Labour's Lost*; it is part of the comic value of the early plays, where Shakespeare lets himself go in the luxury of words. The felicitous game leads us to Act V and the presentation of Nine Worthies to entertain the Princess before she receives the sad news of the death of her father. However, the Princess and Rosaline have their dig at their loves :

Princess : We are wise girls to mock our lovers so.
Rosaline : They are worse fools to purchase mocking so.
(v, ii, 58-59)

Boyet's comment is apposite:

The tongues of mocking wenches are as keen
As is the razor's edge invisible. (V, ii, 257-58)

Holofernes, who had a serious discussion on the killing of deer, obliges Jaquenetta and asks her to take Berowne's letter to Rosaline. Berowne's entry with an unfinished sonnet in hand recalls to us Shakespeare's work on the Sonnets. Shakespeare's dark lady seems to haunt him:

Love's feeling is more soft and sensible
Than are the tender horns of cockled snails.
(IV,iii, 332-33)

But the love-game is on. Those who had sworn to renounce women, entertain them with the Masque of the Nine Worthies. Holofernes and Nathaniel, with the Duke in attendance, indulge in strictures on Don Armado, a representative of upperclass Englishmen of Shakespeare's time. One of the privileges of aristocrats anywhere in the world is to mispronounce words : the Don says "cauf" for "calf", "hauf" for "half" and "nebor" for "neighbour". This is also to make fun of the euphemists of the period. However, the ladies are to be entertained in "the posterior of the day". They receive their love letters and gifts. Rosaline, in love with "Biron", would treat him thus :

> How I would make him fawn, and beg, and seek,
> And wait the season, and observe the times,
> And spend his prodigal wits in bootless rimes,
> And shape his service wholly to my hests. (V, ii, 62-65)

It is all the spirit of "Pair-taunt like" (tit-for-tat) or she will have a hand in beating his winning card.

The portrait suggested above may not be attractive by Elizabethan standards, but perhaps the dark lady, being cultured and sophisticated, might have spoken to herself.

Boyet, "stabbed" with laughter, brings the news that the King and his men will return disguised as "Muscovites or Russians" to pursue their several suits. His account of the men in their pursuit of love adds to the comedy for it is in stark contrast to their behaviour in the early part of the play. Boyet seems to be the favourite of the poet. Berowne describes him with spontaneous wit :

> This fellow pecks up wit, as pigeons pease,
> And utters it again when God doth please.
> ————————————————
> This gallant pins the wenches on his sleeve.
> Had he been Adam, he had tempted Eve.
> (V, ii, 316-17; 322-23)

The playwright is speaking in his own person, and we anticipate the creation of Osric and Le Beau. The King and his companions are transformed into human beings, tempted by love; they are no longer bookmen. The ladies also rise to the occasion : they decide to wear masks and exchange their distinguishing "favours" so that the King will make love to Rusaline and Berowne to the Princess.

On the whole, the reaction to the masque is not favourable. Holofernes sums up : Costard as Pompey and Armado as Hector are not effective. Nathaniel as Alexander, Holofernes as Judas, and moth as Hercules form the cast of the Nine Worthies : "This is not generous, not gentle, not humble" (V, ii, 621). This is a beautiful summary of Shakespeare's view of what is fantastic and nonsensical."

It is time now for love's labour to go in vain, the powerful effect (in the person of Marcade) bringing the sad news of the Princess's father's death, which is announced at the end of Boyet's humorous remark against Armado wearing "a dish-clout of Jaquenetta's and that, wears next his heart for a favour" (V, ii, 702-3)

This is an effective close for a frivolous theme. It is a big surprise that it replaces a normal comic ending. The reality of the situation is indicated in a few words of prose; the bookmen have to continue to forswear women for one more year. But Berowne's words are significant:

> Your beauty, ladies,
> Hath much deformed us, fashioning our humors
> Even to the opposed end of our intents;
> And what in us hath seemed ridiculous—
> As love is full of unbefitting strains,
> All wanton as a child, skipping and vain,
> Formed by the eye and therefore, like the eye,
> Full of straying shapes, of habits and of forms,
> Varying in subjects as the eye doth roll
> To every varied object in his glance. (V,ii,746-55)

Berowne speaks for all lovers. The Princess prescribes "austere and insociable life" for "twelve celestial signs". Hence love must abide its testing. Berowne's observations, although varied, evoke the spirit of the comedy:

> Our wooing doth not end like an old play;
> Jack hath not Jill: These ladies' courtesy
> Might well have made our sport a comedy. (V,ii.864-66)

Although Marcade's word brings a sad note into the comedy, the tenor does not diminish. All the characters have given expression to their innate desire for making love. Shakespeare allows the marriage of Jaquenetta and Armado. The spirit of the play is caught in the magic of the closing songs, sung by all, irrespective of the station to which they belong: King, Princess, courtiers, and local inhabitants all join gently in the chorus of the wintersong, which ends thus: "The words of Mercury are harsh after the songs of Apollo."

1. Robert Spaight, *Shakespeare : The Man and His Achievement*, (London : Dent, 1977), p. 117.
2. Ford Madox Ford, *The English Novel* (London : Dent, 1930), p. 81.

6

A MIDSUMMER NIGHT'S DREAM

In an examination paper, in answer to a question on the central theme of *A Midsummer Night's Dream*, a student wrote that it was the approaching marriage of Theseus and Hippolyta. He also thought that it could be a play about a dream of crossed loves, futile quarrels and searches, and of strange translations happening on a strange day, Midsummer Eve (June 23). The examinee was more than right: in the comedies devoted to love and courtship, this seems to be the obvious answer.

It may have been the wedding of Essex (1590), Derby (1595), or Southampton (1598) that prompted the playwright to make the wedding of Theseus and Hippolyta the core of his play. J.L. Calderwood calls the play "Shakespeare's continuing exploration of the nature, function, and value of art". The mythological material of the valiant hero, Theseus, marrying Hippolyta, Queen of the Amazons, is emphasised in the play besides the arguments of Theseus and Hippolyta—reason as opposed to imagination in the Court of Athens. This is done as a "union and interpretation of the universal and the particular", in Coleridge's description of the excellence of Shakespeare. Diverse materials (elves and spirits, the human and the supernatural) are woven together. "What, wilt thou hear some music, my sweet love ?" (IV, i, 28) says Queen Titania to ass-headed Bottom, with whom she is in love. Many cartoonists, who undervalue the merit of ass-headed Bottom as a man of culture, use the line as a source for caricaturing. Besides, music plays a great part in Shakespeare; it entertains lovers in *The Merchant of Venice*, and it recalls mad Lear to sanity and the statue of Hermione to life. No wonder the transformed Bottom enjoys it. Hence, in this play Shakespeare seems to go against his will to "glance aside to new-found methods and to compounds strange". In *Love's Labour's Lost* he mixes gentle satire with the delineation of human foibles, and these with epithalamiums in *A Midsummer Night's Dream*; but, he warns, "What fools these mortals be!' (III, ii, 115)

The warning comes from Puck, who functions as the comic chorus of the play. Shakespeare takes care to distinguish his young men and women; the girls are distinguished by their spirited personalities: Hermia is dark, while Helena is blonde, given to weeping but pursuing her goal relentlessly; so she shares some of the qualities of the heroines in classical drama. This may be a general comment of Shakespeare on humanity, so beautifully demonstrated in *Love's Labour's Lost*. But the *Dream's* enjoyment lies in its richness, sophistication, and worldly wisdom. If the play was composed for a wedding (and that seems a fact), Shakespeare seems to have had Queen Elizabeth I in mind when he composed Theseus's advice to Hermia :

> To live a barren sister all your life,
> Chanting strange hymns to the cold fruitless moon
> Thrice bless'd they that master so their blood.
> To undergo such maiden pilgrimage;
> But earthlier happy is the rose distilled,
> Than that which withering on the virgin thorn,
> Grows, lives, and dies in single blessedness. (I, i, 72-78)

The queen attended the marriage of William Stanley, Earl of Derby, and Lady Elizabeth, grand-daughter of Lord Burghley and the queen's grand-daughter and maid of honour on 26 January 1595. The only unkind and unchivalrous metaphor compares the queen to a rose "withering on the virgin thorn". Perhaps the queen may not have liked the reference in a play of midsummer performed at a winter wedding.

It is also argued that the play was written for the wedding of the Countess of Southampton to Sir Thomas Heneage, on 2 May 1595, as Shakespeare was a great friend of that House. Theseus makes reference to "the rite of May", which is close to midsummer and not the cold month January. Artisans like Quince, a carpenter; Snug, a tinker; and Starveling, a tailor, must have been familiar faces in Stratford-upon-Avon. All the characters, both human and superhuman, move their own circles of delicate, fragile arenas with merriment and joy, caused by the moon, which wanes and encourages Lysander to sing at Hermia's window, "With feigning voice, verses of feigning love" (V, i, 31).

The full moon image gives a good start to the play of lovers who are enchanted by moonlight. Theseus wants Hermia to marry Demetrius by the next new moon; otherwise, she will claustrate with Lysander, she informs Helena, who has intentions to escape with Hermia the following night:

> To-morrow night, when Phoebe doth behold
> Her silver visage in the wat'ry glass,
> Decking with liquid pearl the bladed grass...
> (A time that lovers' flights doth still conceal)
> Though Athens gates have divised to steal. (I, i, 209-13)

The moon is again used for the evocation of a congenial atmosphere of love. The conflict between Hermia and her father, Egeus, is soon to be resolved. The lovers have to defend themselves against the hostility of Egeus and the authority of Theseus. Hermia pleads, "I would my father look'd but with my eyes" and Theseus's reply is characteristic : "Rather your eyes must with his judgement look" (I, i, 56).

The old and the young naturally do not look alike; old age has problems, and one of them is that of authority. In the opening scene Egeus lectures to assumed Lysander on love as trivial and deceitful and implies that Hermia's love for Lysander has upset the hierarchy. He describes how he has sung, "With feigning voice, verses of feigning love/And stol'n the impression of her fantasy" (I, i, 30-31).

Egeus attacks her falling in love with Lysander. Duke Theseus's advice is, "To you/your father should be as god" (I, i. 47).

His suggestion that she should prefer Demetrius is rightly rejected, and she meekly responds, "I would my father look'd but with my eyes" (I, i, 56).

Elizabethan lovers, unlike the lovers in classical drama, defy their parents; love gives Hermia the authority to defy even the Duke. She is bold and not coy or modest like her counterparts in a classical play. But Theseus is different: his order that she should abide by her father's decision is typical of classical plays involving lovers.

Whatever the condition under the sharp Athenian law, growing, living, and dying in single blessedness, the lovers have their own way in Shakespeare; Hermia and Lysander meet and converse in stylised speech as Berowne and Rosaline do in *Love's Labour's Lost*.

Lysander : How now, my love? Why is your cheek so pale?
How chance the roses these do fade so fast?
Hermia : Belike for want of rain, which I could well
Between them from the tempest of mine eyes.
(I, ii, 128-31)

Thus the love-talk goes on; Hermia tells her lover to "teach our trial patience" and bear "a customary cross". Helena's arrival introduces the complication necessary for a love plot. Her lines are mischievous :

I will go and tell him of fair Hermia's flight.
Then to the wood will he to-morrow night
Pursue her, (I,i, 246-248)

The course of true love does not run smooth; it goes slowly, beset with difficulties. Hermia's speech is one intermingled with the activities of the "rude mechanics" and sophisticated entertainment, involving the Fairy Queen and others and their moonlight revels.

Demetrius pursues Helena, whom he does not love, though he is in search of Hermia and Lysander : "The one I'll slay, the other slayeth me" (II, i, 190). Helena fawns on him: she is a true and faithful lover who wants Demetrius to use her as his "spaniel". She is prepared to be spurned and struck but says only, "Give me leave, (Unworthy as I am) to follow you" (II, i, 204-5).

Later, she says, "We cannot fight for love, as men may do" (II, i, 241), and in so doing she speaks for all women, East and West.

Oberon instructs Puck:

A sweet Athenian lady is in love

With a disdainful youth. Anoint his eyes;
But do it when the next thing he espies
May be the lady. (II, i, 261-64)

There is a harmonius combination of the human beings with the supernatural. Lysander has to "lie further off". Helena and Hermia are "sweet play fellows" and then Lysander lets Helena into the secret of his planned elopement, and the play moves swiftly. Even as Demetrius and Helena run, she pronounces harsh judgment on hereself ("I am as ugly as a bear"), while she allows that her sweet fellow, Hermia, "hath attractive eyes". But the confusion has set in, and Lysander awakes to find himself in love with Helena. This experience is achieved within the range of artifice:

The will of man is by his reason swayed,
And reason says you are the worthier maid,
Things growing are not ripe until their season;
So, I, being young, till now ripe not to reason.
And touching now the point of human skill,
Reason becomes the marshal to my will
And leads me to your eyes. (II, ii. 115-21)

Helena is taken aback :

Wherefore was I to this been mockery born?
When at your hands did I deserve this scorn ? (II, ii, 123-24)

The interrogatives flash their own answers; she is formal, sententious, and appallingly surprised. Helena is exhausted from her pursuit of Demetrius, and the situation in which Lysander declares his love is comical. The dialogue between Lysander and Helena in the changed circumstances brings out her frustration, her anger, and even astonishment. Helena's verse speaks for itself;

O, that a lady, of one man refused,
Should of another therefore be abused! (II,ii, 133-34)

Act II closes with Hermia waking up after her dream about a

serpent eating her heart away.

Her appealing to Lysander is in keeping with the playful, romantic tenor of the play. In Act II the love affairs of the immortals are at work; Titania claims that she must be the lady of Oberon, but Oberon plays "pipes of corn, and versing love/ To amorous Phillida'' (II,ii, 66-67). The bouncing Amazon was his "husband-mistress" and his "warrier love". Titania has Theseus "through the glimmering night/From perigenia, whom he ravished" (II, i, 77-78).

Titania has persuaded him to break these other "bed-vows" and describes them as "the forgeries of jealousy". But all is fair in love and war; they forget each other's infidelities and Oberon, who shows solicitude for other people's love affairs, and Puck, who wants to see "delight in chaos", arrange things for others. The little Indian boy whom, Titania has brought up, Oberon demands as henchman. She refuses and Oberon wants to take his revenge. He is invisible and he can overhear the conference of Demetrius and Helena. When Puck comes back with the "little western flower", Helena pursues Demetrius, her love unrequited, and Oberon takes pity on her and instructs Puck to drop the juice of "love-in-idleness" into the eye of Demetrius, whom he will recognise "by the Athenian garments he hath on". But Oberon is unware that Lysander is dressed similarly and is wandering in the woods. Puck mistakes his man. Lysander, awaking, sees Helena (exhausted from her pursuit of Demetrius) and declares his love for her. He says:

> Not Hermia, but Helen I love:
> Who will not change a raven for a dove ?
> The will of man is by his reason sway'd
> And reason says you are the worthier maid. (II, ii, 113-16)

Lysander's speech is ironic, for his passion for Helena is unreasonable. It is all very neat now; Helena is in love with Demetrius, Demetrius is in love with Hermia, Lysander is in love with Helena, and Hermia is in love with Lysander. Titania falls in love with ass-headed Bottom. Bottom's comment is true : "reason and love keep little company together now-a days."

Bottom's translation into an ass does him good: he is no longer only Bottom but a gentleman who talks with great charm to fairies; his talk even resembles that of fairies. He tells Mustardseed: "I know your patience well. The same cowardly, giant like ox-beef hath devoured many a gentleman of your house...I desire you of more acquaintance" (III, i, 177-81).

As far as his translation goes, he is a charming lover, quite at home in the company of the fairies. He is superb as a lover who will engage Peter Quince to write a ballad of dreams: "It shall be called 'Bottom's Dream', because it hath no bottom". Shakespeare has discreetly woven the fragile web of the lovers.

In the world of love and dream, Puck's mission has not been as exact of Ariel in *The Tempest*. Puck has laid the love-juice on the wrong pair of eyes, and hence Demetrius pursues Helena. Puck observes "fate overrules" and makes a profound philosophic statement on behalf of his creator: "Lord, what fools these mortals be!"

Mortals make mistakes; they are ruled by a power above, and Oberon tries to keep up the fun by pouring juice on the eyes of Demetrius, who wakes to find himself passionately in love with Helena. Hermia accuses Demetrius of killing Lysander in his sleep: "If thou hast slain Lysander in his sleep/ Being o'er shoes in blood, plunge in knee deep" (III, ii, 46-47). The speech, in rhymed couplets makes the dream of love enchanting. When Hermia appears, the confusion becomes worse confounded and the lovers can see clearly whether Lysander is annointed with "love-in-idleness".

> . . . Robin, overcast the night.
> With drooping fog as black as Acheron. (III, ii, 357-9)

These are the instructions of Oberon; Lysander has fallen asleep, worn out from this desperate blindman's buff with Demetrius. Titania, who is passionately in love with Bottom, is prepared to give up the Indian boy to Oberon; one attachment makes her give up another. All this must be done before the shining of "Aurora's harbinger". But the fairies are familiar with the "morning love". Before the dawn they must vanish into their native empyrean until moonlight and candlelight in conjunction summon them to the "great chamber", so the play continues. Queen Titania has to be woken up and has to change her love for Oberon.

Although *A Midsummer Night's Dream* was written for an occasion, it is a skilful play in which the worlds of the natural and the supernatural mingle. It is very close to Kalidas's *Megadhuta*, or *Cloud Messenger*. Supernatural elements combine with human elements to give us a play of "imagination all compact" and a play-within-a-play in Athens. One endorses Coleridge's remarks on the play: "Very Anacrean in perfectness, proportion, grace, and spontaneity". He also draws our attention to the quality of English fantasy contained in the play. The fairy world constitutes the secondary plot.

The pattern of all the early comedies seems to be uniform: the commentary on the love-making is a happy but serious celebration of multiple weddings in a world of poetry and moonlight "filled with pomp, with triumphs, and with revelling". Titania's love is addressed to a hearer; while Bottom philosophises. Speed and Launce comment on the love of their master and the ladies of France mock at the style of the men courting them.

In keeping to the spirit of the comedy, Theseus and Hippolyta begin the play of celebration of their "nuptial hour", the opening scene inspired by North's *Plautarch* and perhaps by Chaucer's "The Knight's Tale". Theseus tells Philostrate to "Stir up the Athenian young to merriments" (I,i, 12). Philostrate is thus a sort of public-relations officer. The lovers are like figures in a puppet play: they are delicate and respond to the arrows of Cupid. In the world of romance and innocence, Bottom and Titania represent the most striking image of what is to happen in the play. Their contract of union emphasises the desperate elements: the world of humans (Lysander and Demetrius in love with Hermia) is fused with that of the fairies. Oberon (more an Oriental figure) seems to have come from Lord Berners's translation of *Huon of Brodeaux* and Puck (the earth demon or pixy of Irish folkore) resembles Robin Goodfellow. But the most important aspect of the play is Theseus's speech and Hippolyta's reply in the begnning of Act V, after the lovers' "dream" and before the interlude of Pyramus and Thisbe, for Theseus rather foolishly associates the lovers' imagination with that of the poet and the lunatic. This indicates the contrasting attitude of Theseus and Hippolyta in their responses to the lovers' story of the night.

Theseus adheres to reason, as opposed to the imagination. He's worried:

> That is hot ice and wondrous strange snow.
> How shall we find the concord of this discord ? (V, i, 59-60)

It is difficult to agree with Marco Mineoff[3] that Theseus is a choric figure. No doubt he stands for sanity, reason, and commonsense in this world of midsummer madness-and ultimately in his unswerving love for Hippolyta. In a play of this sort, where fancy rules, one fights shy of taking sides either for or against reason. Theseus's rationalism does not diminish the value of poetic imagination; the poet is not exactly like a madman. When the imagination is given a free play, Theseus comes very close to the lover who acts under heat and excitement. The lover's promises are not to be taken very seriously. This is a universal phenomenon. When Kalidasa's lovers break their promise, the curse of Durvasa comes to the rescue of the husband. Shakespeare's views are really implicit and not quite clear. Theseus's position is in the stage of exploration. In a way, Hippolyta tries to supplement Theseus's views. Some of us belong to a civilisation different from that of the playwright and believe in dreams, whether Freudian in substance or not, which are not always of never-sleeping imagination. They foretell and even warn. However, the dream is ephemeral and cannot last long. Bottom, who is now transformed, can appreciate music: "Let us have the tongs and bones". This cannot go on too long. Titania must be woken up and Bottom must be discarded. This happens before the strains of music die down and Titania is wondering how she was found "with those mortals on the ground" (IV, i, 104). Theseus's hunting horns have told us that "we are now in "The vanguard of the day" and the lovers under the charm will wake to their right minds. Everyone behaves normally. Theseus, charmed by the "gentle concord" between the rival claimants to Egeus's daughter, Hermia, allows "the couples externally be knit".

It is interesting to comment on Bottom, who has slept the soundest and awakes to find that the others have gone: "I have had a dream, past the whit of man to say what dream it was. Man is but an ass if he go about to expound this dream...I will get Peter Quince to write a ball of this dream. It shall be called Bottom's dream, because it hath no bottom" (IV, i, 207-8; 211-13). He is aware that "The play's the thing", while all are still recovering. Bottom (with the ass's head), who has slept with the Queen of the Fairies, comes into his own quickly and says most sensible things. He tells his colleagues, "And, most dear actors, eat no onions nor garlic, for we are to utter sweet breath; and I do not doubt but to hear them say it is a sweet comedy" (IV, ii, 37-40), a dream of beatific vision from which he recovers quickly and about which he speaks realistically.

Act V, which forms the conclusion of the play, deals with the most important event for which the readers and audience are anxiously awaiting. The rehearsal of "Pyramus and This-be" poetry and drama create illusion. Theseus's prologue says, "All for your delight. We are not here" (V, i, 114-15).

The actors rehearse their parts before the actual performance: the short dialogue between Hippolyta and Theseus is a commentary on the aesthetics of a play. It points to Hamlet's instruction to the players later in Shakespeare's dramatic career.

Hippolyta : This is the silliest stuff that ever I heard.

Theseus : The best in this kind are but shadows' and the worst are no worse, if imagination amend them.

Hippolyta : It must be your imagination then, and not theirs.

Theseus : If we imagine no worse of them than they of themselves, they may pass for excellent men. Here come two noble beasts in, a man and a lion. (V, i, 211-217)

Shakespeare, the up-and-coming playwright, is already musing on the nature of his profession.

The lover's experience in the forest is chaotic; it is not like that of the lovers in the Forest of Arden. The play, which weaves between patterned language and rhymed couples comes back to normality. Finally, harmony is created; it is seen in the working-out of a dance pattern; and the play's objectives are fulfilled : "Jack shall have Jill: nought shall go ill", or, as, "The man shall have his mate again, and all shall be well" (III, ii, 46).

This is in keeping with Puck's lines that close the play of friendship and love:

> Give me your hands, if we be friends,
> And Robin shall restore amends. (V, i, 426-27)

A Midsummer Night's Dream is a delightful play of human beings and fairies: mortal and immortal worlds meet and separate; they do not brush but collide. When the fairies perform their dance of blessing at the end, the mortals return to their concentric routine. In this respect, it is very close to Kalidasa's *Shakuntala*, in which the dramatic events move because of the intervention of gods.

NOTES

1. Marco Mincoff, *Shakespeare: Select Bibliographical Guides* (Oxford : 1973), p. 69.

7

THE MERCHANT OF VENICE

A Midsummer Night's Dream has been the most popular of all Shakespeare's plays in India; it has the features of a festival drama: it is highly fantastic and has a combination of human and supernatural figures. All this has been achieved deliberately, preventing a picture of the tragic side of life. There are folklore elements, too, with fate vastly more important than will. Fairies from folklore commingle with deities from ancient mythology. Dance, mythology, nonsense, philosophy, and absurdity in colloquial prose and verse bring the play very close to the Sanskrit of Sudraka.

But *the Merchant of Venice*, which also avoids tragédy, is more intellectual and realistic and sometimes strains our credibility. It, too, is often on the boards in India, and it also contains folk elements. It appeals to the audience of the classical theatre because of the character the Jew: he represents "the greediness of worldly choosers and bloody mind of users". In the process there is the sacrifice of friendship, and a display of loyalty, generosity, and nobility. Money-lending is a universal phenomenon. Besides, the stories of the bond and flesh and the casket choice seem to be universal.

Stories resembling Shylock's "merry bond" are found in Indian classical epics. In the *Mahabharatha* (2000-500 BC) is found the story of the noble king Sibira, who cut off flesh from his body to save a dove from a falcon and in the process of weighing it said that he was prepared to give up his whole body. This pleased the gods, who wanted to test his sense of charity; and the two birds revealed themselves as Indra and Agni, the gods of Indian mythology. There is no legal quibble here, and the story of Shylock does not go as far, "Censor Mundi", the fourteenth-century, poem, also contains myths and legends of the kind, including a flesh bond. In *Gesta Romanorum* occurs the bond theme linked with the tale of wooing. The arguments seem to be echoed in Shakespeare.

Shakespeare has given a distinct place for the play to begin—Venice. His Venice has a character; it is a seaport and reminds one of a modern city of business and enterprise. The sea holds all the fortunes of Antonio. Here are all the main characters, except Shylock's daughter, Jessica, a sort of Proserpine in the world of Pluto. Padua is the world of females, of love and of courting, bathed in moonlight that helps the evocation of atmosphere conducive to the lovers; one even hears the music of the spheres at the end of the play, which has abundant references to metals—gold, silver and lead. It is a lovely dream that offers a bride "richly left" fabulous gambler's luck, fortunes repaired at the expenses of usurers, and the law transformed from a nose around one's neck to the agent of a good fairy:

> Fair ladies, you drop manna in the way
> Of starved people. (V, i, 293-94)

One endorses this statement of Lorenzo.

Here's God's plenty, as Dryden was to say, for young lawyers. The trial, for Essex, must have provided a reminder of how he wrung confessions out of the wretched Jewish physician Dr. Lopez (who was executed on the charges of attempting to poison the queen), and for Southampton a chance to unlearn the lesson of Tennyson's Northern Farmer: "Don't thee marry for for money, but for where money is." There is much talk about usury, property, and wealth, and a healthy concern with money in Shakespeare, for a kind of dowry system existed in Elizabethan society. The nurse in *Romeo and Juliet* boasts, "He that marries her shall have the chinks."

There are other topical problems in the play, especially corruption in Court society: and any suggestion about the greatest lottery of all, presided over by the ageing Fairy Queen, was as likely to break a man as to make him. Essex was ruined by Queen Elizabeth when he referred to renewing his "farming" of the tax on sweet wine. Perhaps, in the character of Shylock, Shakespeare is portraying Southampton, who was reduced to selling his family estates. Those were the days when a rich marriage was a form of "heavy rescue" work.

Shylock, who dominates the first half of the play, becomes a victim at the end.

One need not agree with Granville-Barker's assertion that "There is no more reality in Shylock's bond and the Lord of Belmont's will than in Jack and the Bean stalk". There are some characters (Salerio and Salanio, for example who are not dramatically effective but can sense the danger that befalls Antonio. However, in the opening scene, they help establish Antonio, who is suffering from sadness, which wearies him. The opening, which is reminiscent of *Twelfth Night*, is very effective. Antonio says:

And such a want-wit sadness makes of me,
That I have much ado to know myself. (I, i, 6-7)

It is Salerio and Solanio who keep up the tempo of the early scenes and help Antonio play a part (and this "a sad one") till the arrival of Bassanio, Gratiano, and Lorenzo). It is not right to read too much of our reaction to characters into a play; they are circumscribed within an artificial boundary; hence it "is not right to see Portia as trying to create suspense to become a dramatic triumph with herself at the centre"[2]. Her play-acting seems dramatic, although one could express the doubt whether Bassanio might not have recognised Portia, Gratiano, and Nerissa. There are critics who find fault with Antonio for not resisting Shylock's claim, as his death could demonstrate his love for Bassanio. This seems to me a misreading, because even in the classical epic adherence to law or truth is vital. King Sibira does not protest; he willingly allows himself to be cut into pieces. Protest or resistance goes against the ethical code, at least in the Eastern epic. However, in a play which borders on credibility, Coleridge's advice that willing suspension of disbelief is the essence of poetic truth comes in handy.

The *Merchant of Venice* is a comedy of rich, dramatic strands, well-woven, that moves easily between the places of merchandise and of love. But amid love of wealth and merchandise there is also a great friendship between Antonio and Bassanio, who says: "To you, Antonio I owe the most in money and love" (I, i, 130-31).

It is a great story of friendship, of Bassanio's guileless days. Therefore, he unburdens his heart to Antonio and tells of his interest in Portia, "a lady richly left".

This intimate friendship, documented in the opening scene, is misinterpreted by the Freudians, who need not be taken seriously. But soon the play moves to highlight Shylock, who dominates the first part of the play and has a long ancestry in drama. He stems from Marlowe's Barabas of *The Jew of Malta*, a play in which Shakespeare may have acted. But Shylock is more human than Barabas. His portrait emerges very impressive; he is not to be read as a central character in a conflict between Jews and the Christians: it is as mistaken a view as that Caliban is a symbol of exploitation in *The Tempest*. This is a red herring and not an accurate account of Shakespeare's attitude to semitism and colonialism, which perhaps were not great matters of interest in those days. But the portraiture of Shylock enables the playwright to train his hand in future depictions of tragic heroes. Shylock emerges a near-tragic hero. In lines I, ii, 3-10, which resemble the *Stichomythia* of a Greak play, Shylock is established in the mind of the readers and audience. His idiom, his views, and his attitude show that he has Antonio under his control. He is aware of the potential richness of his prospective client : "The man is... sufficient" (I, iii, 24). He is a man of strong views and convictions who would have earned the appreciation of the Elizabethan audience when he declares, "I will buy with you, sell with you, talk with you, walk with you, but I will not eat with you, drink with you, nor pray with you" (I, iii, 31-35). These words are in good Elizabethan prose; but soon, on seeing Antonio, in an aside in simple and effective blank verse, Shylock declaims,

How like a fawning publican he looks.
I hate him for he is a Christian. (I, iii, 37-38)

Shylock is built on the figure of the Puritan usurer, who was familiar with the code of the Old Testament. It is true that the Christians did not recognise Jews as members of the human race, and hence Shylock's outburst, 'Hath not a Jew eyes...?" Antonio, who neither lends nor borrows, breaks a custom to "supply the ripe wants" of Bassanio. Antonio has no respect for Shylock ("a villain with a smiling cheek"; "A goodly apple rotten at the heart"). Like money-lenders all over the world, Shylock has made money breed as fast as Jacob's earnings; he has borne the insults of Antonio at the Rialto patiently, and he is now ready to "catch him upon the hip", and is prepared to seal a single bond "in a merry sport" whose condition is abominable. It runs:

> let the forfeit
> Be nominated for an equal pound
> Of your fair flesh, to be cut off and taken
> In what part of your body pleaseth me. (I, iii, 144-47)

This is strongly reminiscent of the story of King Sibira in the *Mahabharata*. The Jews were the rejected ones; infidels had "Jewish hearts". Sometimes the treachery of the Christians can be very theatrical; social conflicts have always been the favourites of the dramatists. Shylock is deprived of Old Gobbo's present of a dish of doves. He is a cruel master. Launcelot Gobbo says, "Give him a present ? Give him a halter; I am famished in his service" (II, ii, 97-99). As a father, Shylock has not earned the affection of his daughter, Jessica, who tells Launcelot, "Our house is hell, and thou a merry devil" (II, ii, 195). She is ready to become a Christian and Lorenzo's loving wife. Shakespeare develops a tone to suit the harsh nature of Shylock, who alternates in love and hate:

> What, Jessica!—Thou shall not gormandize
> As thou hast done with me;—What, Jessica!
> And sleep, and snore, and rend apparel out.
> Why, Jessica, I say! (II, v, 3-6)

These lines of alliteration have the echoes of Marlowe, who breaks up the lines to gain in intensity and develops conversational tones in the dialogue of his plays. Soon they change to a mood of hesitancy when he hands in the keys to Jessica and asks her to take care to see that "shallow fippery" shall not enter his "sober house". His heart breaks when he hears that Jessica spent four ducats in Genoa. When he loses his jewels, ducats, and Jessica, he raves madly, but of a turquoise found on one of Antonio's creditors, he says, "I had it of Leah when I was a bachelor" (III, i, 110-11). Shakespeare does not seem to lose sight of essential humanity, even when an individual is stone-hearted.

In the trial scene, the Jew (who earlier uttered, "If you prick us, do we not bleed?") reaches the depth of hatred in superb blank verse:

> I have sworn an oath that I'll have my bond.
> Thou call'dst me dog before thou hadst a cause,
> But since I am a dog, beware my fangs. (III, iii, 5-8)

Behind these lines of revenge is the hatred of Antonio and his company, the abduction of his daughter, and the loss of money. He is obsessed with the bond, which is reinforced by the simple half-line "I'll have my bond", repeated three times. The antagonism between Shylock and Antonio is clearly documented at first on the rising wave-length. Shylock is dignified, although he does not respond to Antonio's "bootless prayers". Act IV is very theatrically constructed. Antonio is reconciled ("Let me have judgment, and the Jew his life"), but Shylock insists, "I stand here for the law", and the mercy pleas of Portia fall on his deaf ears: "I crave the law, The penalty and forfeit of my bond" (IV, i, 203-04).

Shakespeare's mind is preoccupied with the positive law of equity in the dealings of man with man, and he had already made references to it in the Sonnets and was to take it up in *King Lear*, *Hamlet*, *Measure for Measure*, and *The Winter's Tale*. One aspect of equity that is elaborated in the tragedies is the conflicting system of revenge and charity within the framework of the law. Eastern epic writers would insist (even if the bond is oral) on the fulfilment of the promise, and hope that finally a miracle will happen and reward those who are faithful. But here Shakespeare insists on the provisions of the "merry bond", a fallacious one, and averts the tragedy by a legal quibble. But the dramatic episode is made up of a surprise in which the tables are turned on Shylock. But for Shylock, the bond has religious connotations. He tells Tubal, "Go, Tubal, fee me an officers...I will have the heart of him if he forfeit...Go, Tubal, meet me at our synagogue". He rejects Antonio's plea on the score that he has sworn an oath and that he will have his bond. This is reinforced at the trial (III, i, 110-14).

> I have possessed your Grace of what I purpose,
> And by our holy Sabbath have I sworn
> To have the due and forfeit of my bond. (IV, i, 35-37)

This is a tone of hatred and revenge, but Victor Hugo thought it was "consecrated...sacerdotal".

A normal student of drama is interested in the way the trial scene develops. Portia, who dominates the trial scene, when Shylock refuses a tender on "open court", asks him whether Antonio is unable to repay the principal. When Bassanio offers to pay twice the sum due, Shylock insists on his bond. Portia's clever quibble on the spilling of blood turns the arguments against Shylock. Although the scene is full of ambiguities, they are for the lawyers; it is an enjoyable scene in which Shylock is reduced to pieces. His excitement, his exclamation, "A Daniel come to judgment", vanishes in a moment, and he leaves the court sad and tragic when it is declared that Shylock is not entitled to even the principal but only to "justice and his bond". It is Gratiano's turn to mock: "A Daniel still say I, a second Daniel!" (IV, i, 337). As an alien in Venice, he is further humiliated: his property is seized and given over to Lorenzo and Jessica and he exits as a fallen man:

> I pray you give me leave to go home from hence;
> I am not well. Send the deed after me,
> And I'll sign it (IV, i, 394-96)

Although the play can be seen as a balance between mercy and justice, according to Nevill Coghill the judgment cannot be taken as a punishment for Shylock's sin of avarice. His treatment releases a resentment of unmerited injuries and unceremonious dismissal at the hands of Antonio and his friends. It goes even deeper than this. With Shylock's departure, the fairy story moves towards concord and peace, with only minor obstacles.

Portia is one of the very clever young heroines cast in the mould of the women of the romances who do not make mistakes in their lives. In her dealing with suitors she is business-like. She is bound by duty to choose, "by the manner of my father's will". She deals coldly with Morocco, who is apologetic: "Mislike me not for my complexion."

Prince Arragon goes by the literal description of the superscription on the casket. Both lose, and only Bassanio can succeed. The choice of the right casket is like that in the Eastern epics, in selecting a prince from among many. After the trial the play moves quickly on the path of love, culminating in a double wedding. Bassanio, in some ways luckier than Antonio, is a high-spirited, pleasure-loving suitor in search of dowry. Antonio's part in the world is destined to be a sad one, for he is described as "a tainted wether of the flock". One whose purse is ever open to Bassanio and prepared to share in his happiness. He emerges a pale antagonist to Shylock, but he is generous with his money and he is a big tradesman, with his ships off the shores of Tripoli, the Indies, Mexico, and England. If there is a shipwreck, Salario imagines:

Which touching but my gentle vessel's side
Would scatter all her spices on the stream,
Enrobe the roaring waters with my silks. (I, i, 31-34)

The lyricism of Act V, scene i is a fitting close to this fairy tale. It is full of allusions: all great and genuine lovers are recalled.

……in such a night
Troilus methinks mounted the Troyan walls,
And sigh'd his soul toward Grecian tents,
Where Cressid lay that night. (V, i, 3-6)

Thisbe, Dido, and Medea are great names in the romances; to that list is added the name of Jessica. Other names that could be added are Portia and Nerissa. The climax is the wedding, of which Stephano brings the news :

My mistress will before the break of day

> Be here at Belmont. She doth stray about
> By holy crosses where she kneels and prays
> For happy wedlock hours. (V, i, 29-32)

There is much music in the air. Shakespeare, who often uses music for occasions of joy, uses the opportunity to speak on its efficacy:

> The man that hath no music in himself,
> Nor is not moved with concern of sweet sounds,
> Is fit for treasons, strategems, and spoils;
> The motions of his spirit are dull as night,
> And his affections dark as Erebus.
> Let no such man be trusted. (V, i, 83-88)

The attempt to create an atmosphere of music and joy is a little disturbed by the rings' episode. Testing the fidelity of their husbands, Portia and Nerissa fill the fifth act with their long speeches on virtue, and soon the atmosphere of joy is restored and the discovery of the rings brings them together.

The world of *The Merchant of Venice* is a world of money, friendship, prejudice, love, and culture. Although it emphasises that "money is a medium of exchange," Shakespeare hints at other values—friendship and love—that are more enduring.

NOTES

1. Harley Granville-Barker, *Prefaces to Shakespeare* Princeton, N.J. ; Princeton University Press, 1952, p. 355.
2. Sir Arthur Quiller-Couch, Introduction to the New Cambridge Edition of *The Merchant of Venice* (1962), p. xviii.
3. According to the Arden edition, when Alan McKinnon produced the play at the Garrick Theatre in 1905, he had Antonio and Bassanio hold the stage at the final curtain. This is a complete misreading of the play, and Shakespeare's Portia would not like to be assigned the position of a Victorian doormat wife or a meek Indian wife.

8

THE MERRY WIVES OF WINDSOR

The Merry Wives of Windsor, in more ways than one, is the closest of Shakespeare's early comedies to a classical comedy, for it is the one in which domestic intrigues dominate. One more interested in purse than in love and purity tries to lure married women away from the path of virtue. Wives trying to hide their lovers (to save themselves from embarrassment) is a common theme in Eastern plays. The Falstaff of *The Merry Wives*, even if he is not as authentic as in the history plays, reminds one of the Vidhushaka of classical Indian plays though he will hesitate to make love to grown, married women. His background is more orthodox. Falstaff, who stands out in the galaxy of Shakespeare's comic characters, is admirable, whether he makes love for money or for lust. He gives the play its remarkable quality. Queen Elizabeth was so pleased with his part in *Henry IV* that she commanded Shakespeare to continue him in one more play and to show him in love. John Dennis, the literary critic of the early nineteenth century, was also of the view that the play was written in response to the Queen's eagerness, and the playwright finished it in fourteen days.

This theme of domestic comedy is in the English tradition; though the setting is in England, the technique derives from Italian comedy. Whatever may be the present views about the composition of the play, the virgin Queen perhaps regarded love as a punishment, an affliction (and indeed it is so described by the master of love, Ovid). She may have wished to take vengeance on Falstaff on behalf of all chaste women. John Dennis's dedication of *The Comical Gallant* (1702) to George Granville comments on the play thus:

> That this Comedy was not despicable, I gess'd for several Reasons; First, I knew very well, that it has plac'd one of

the greatest Queens that ever was in the World, great not only for her Wisdom in the Arts of Government, but for her knowledge of Polite Learning, and her nice taste of the Drama, for such a taste we may be sure she had, by the relish which she had of the Ancients. This Comedy was written at her command and by her direction, and she was so eager to see it Acted, that she commanded it to be finished in fourteen days; and was afterwards, as Tradition tells, as, very well pleas'd at the representation.

Falstaff's ill-judged interest in Mistress Ford and Mistress Page derives as much from cupidity as from passion. In 1709 Rowe, Shakespeare's first biographer, also thought that the play was written in response to a Royal Command. In 1710 Gildon wrote that "the Fairys in the fifth act make a handsome complement to the Queen, in her palace of Windsor". There is also a theory that the play was written for the Garter Feast in 1597. The play was a great hit after the Restoration in 1660. People who saw the production in the Vere Street Theatre on 5 December 1660 thought "the humour of the country gentleman presumably Slender and the French doctor very well done" but did not think much of the role of Cartwright's Falstaff and the rest. The play has the distinction of having been used for the librettos of a number of musical works, including Verdi's *Falstaff* (1893) and Nicola's *The Merry Wives of Windsor* (1879). It shows that comic domestic situations have their permanent appeal.

Whatever may be the source of *The Merry Wives*, it is read and enjoyed as Shakespeare's only domestic comedy in the Italian tradition and set in England. It is a comedy of ordinary middle-class people, of whom the two wives emerge chaste and happy after all the advances made by Falstaff. Falstaff and his merry cronies, red-nosed Bardolph, Nym (who abuses words) and Pistol (who is fond of quotations from earlier drama) form the centre of interest. Falstaff (who does not appear to be infatuated, but is a victim of incurable "cousumption of the purse") does not emerge as clever as the merry wives: Mistress Ford and Mistress Page are more lively and interesting than their lover.

Sir John Falstaff, who rightly heads the list of *dramatis*

personae, is important in the play, but he is not what he was in the two parts of *Henry IV*. He is no longer looked upon as a humorous, beer-swigging, fat but witty young man who misguided the King, but as one who is fond of purse. Justice Shallow, in his opening speech, tells Slender: "If he were twenty Sir John Falstaffs he shall not abuse Robert Shallow, Esquire" (1,1,2-3). When he arrives, he is accompanied by his followers, the red-nosed crony Bardolph, Nym, and Pistol ("Cony-catching rascals all"), and by Shallow, whom he has hurt by beating his men, killing his deer, and breaking open his lodge. Sir Hugh Evans, a Welsh parson, is the peacemaker.

There is no love in Falstaff, and one does not like to forgive his follies. He is very unsuccessful, very cunning, and not an intellectual. In the Garter Inn at Windsor, where he has installed himself with his disreputable followers, he is a nuisance to everybody. His host tells him, "speak scholarly and wisely", but his response is least scholarly: "I must turn away some of my followers". His love letter to Mistress Page, which begins Act II, is composed with vivacity: "Ask me no reason why I love you". Mistress Page (as a mother of a grown-up daughter) is shocked getting any such letter at all. She says, "I will exhibit a bill in the parliament for the putting down of men" (II,i, 26-27).

This comic incongruity stems from Falstaff's writing a similar letter to Mistress Ford who exchanges notes with her friend, Mrs. Page. Mrs. Ford declares, "I think the best way were to entertain him with hope till the wicked fire of lust have melted him in his own grease" (II,i,60-62). The old goat, not being an adept in writing love letters, has not changed anything in the letter to Mrs. Ford except the name: "I warrant he hath a thousand of these letters, writ with blank space for different names". But both women are determined: "Let's be revenged on him". Pistol, who is a sort of an informer, tells Mr. Ford of Falstaff's love for his wife: "He woos both high and low, both rich and poor". However, the women's determination to encourage Falstaff in his amorous dealing helps us judge Falstaff as a lover. It is good to study him as a lover who learns by experience. He tells Mistress Quickly, "getting the attraction of my good parts aside, I have no other charms". He becomes an easy victim to Ford's design. Ford describes him as a damned Epicurean rascal (II,ii,259). Ford as Master Brook, is a comic, jealous man: "God be praised for my jealousy," says he after having encouraged Falstaff to go to his wife at eleven o' clock. This provides the comic incongruity. He is convinced that his wife will be untasteful to him. Falstaff tells Ford (as Brook), "I shall be with her between ten and eleven; for at that time the jealous rascally knave her husband will be forth" (II,ii,237-40). At the right moment, Ford says, "Our revolted wives share damnation together". (III,ii,35).

In this scene Falstaff's wit triumphs over Mrs. Page's information that Ford is arriving with "half Windsor at the heels" to search for a friend, and she makes him get into her wash basket and both women cover him with foul linen. Mistress Ford had carefully prepared her trap for Falstaff. This is a very broad farcical situation. He feels sad: "Have I lived to be carried in like a barrow of butcher's offal and to be thrown in the Thames?" If he had died by drowning, his body would have swelled like a mountain. But he falls a victim again to Mrs. Ford's trick. His wit comes into its own when Ford comes back as Master Brook. He describes his amorous adventures with his wife: "After we had embraced, kissed, protested and, as it were, spoke this prologue of our comedy" (III,v, 66-67). The merry women play their roles charmingly. Mistress Page speaks just loudly enough so that Falstaff can hear her to be friendly and yet to be very startled when she learns that he is at the house, suggesting the device of the washing basket as the best way for him to escape. The fat man hides in buck-basket, where he had the experience of smell, which offended his nostrils.

Wit and intelligence come into their own in his description of his predicament in his basket. This does not teach him a lesson, for he is again prepared to act as a lover and is sent out dressed in the maid's aunt's dress. He is confident, tells Ford (Brook) again that he went to Mrs. Ford like "a poor old man and came from her like a poor old woman; for in the shape of man, Master Brook, I fear not Goliath with a weaver's beam, because I know also life is a shuttle"(V,i,18-21). He is sure of having Mrs. Ford; self delusion is strong in Falstaff. This aspect of the play links him to several characters in *Twelfth Night*. In the last attempt of his illusion he appears as

Herne, with a buck's head on, in Windsor Park where Mrs. Ford and Mrs. Page appear to befriend him. He is joined by Sir Hugh Evans, as a satyr and Pistol as a hobgoblin, Anne Page and the Fairy Queen, attended by her brother and other fairies with waxen papers on their heads. This is the "grande affaire". Anne Page's description of the elves reminds one of the knights of the Garter being invested in St. George's Chapel, Windsor. The Falstaff-Ford-Brook story is common to Eastern epics in which a lover unwittingly tells of the progress of an affair with the husband's wife. Anne Page, who dominates the last act, invokes the elves:

Search Windsor Castle, elves, within and out.
Strew good luck, ouphs on every sacred room,
That it may stand till the perpetual doom,
In state as wholesome as in state 'tis fit,
Worthy the owner, and the owner it.
The several chairs of order look you scour
With juice of balm and every precious flower:
Each fair instalement, coat, and several crest,
With loyal blazon, evermore be blest,
And nightly, meadow-fairies, look you sing,
Like to the Garter's compass, in a ring. (V,v,54-65)

Of course, the elves are metaphorical, and the speech is a clear reference to the annual ceremony at which the knights take their places, each in his own stall and under his own canopy, in St. George's Chapel. The playwright sums up the mirth in a dumb show, and:

[During this song the Fairies pinch Falstaff. Doctor]
[Caius comes one way, and steals away a Fairy in
green; Slender] another way, and takes off a Fairy
in white; and Fenton, comes, and steals away Anne Page
A noise of hunting is heard within. The Fairies run
away. Falstaff pulls off his buck's head and rises.
(V,v,109-10)

Very soon Falstaff is pinched for interfering with the Windsor wives. The whole illusion of Falstaff depends on Ford's comic jealousy, which is ably dramatised by the playwright.

Besides the merry wives and Falstaff, we have a host of characters belonging to the middle class, who provide strength to the comedy. In this context, Elizabeth gave Shakespeare a deadline: she obviously wanted the play for a special occasion of investiture of the new Kinights of the Garter at Windsor on 24 May 1596. Shakespeare, with the other Lord Chamberlain's men, may have attended the ceremony in "blue coats faced with orange-coloured taffeta and orange-coloured feathers in their hats, most parts having chains of gold".

Anne Page—the pretty daughter of Page, whom Sir Hugh Evans wants to marry to his cousin, Abraham Slender, a strutting fool with a little yellow beard, who is sponsored by her father—is the central female character in the plot. Her position gives rise to a number of humorous situations. All marriages in the play seem to be contracted on the one criterion—wealth. Evans knows that she has seven hundred pounds of money, and gold and silver. Slender, as his name indicates, cannot keep his end of a conversion without his book of riddles, which he unfortunately lends to Alice Shortcase just before Michaelmas, and Parson Evans knows that it will not be easy to persuade Anne to marry Slender. He tells Nym, "I am not altogether an ass," but he is prepared to marry Anne upon any reasonable demands. He wants to use mistress Quickly to help him in winning the hand of Anne. Mistress Quickly is a blithering old dame who can undertake any sort of matchmaking. She boasts, "Never a woman of Windsor knows more of Anne's mind than I do." But Anne's heart is for Fenton, a young gentleman from London, though the French Doctor Caius is also courting her. Mistress Quickly (although she knows that Fenton has a good heart) says, "I would my master had Mistress Anne; or I would Fenton had her. I will do what I can for them all three" (III, iv,100-103). Doctor Caius challenges Mistress Quickly to a duel, which indeed is comic. Anne is in a field near Windsor, waiting with drawn rapier for the person, who never comes. Caius waits in another field, near Frogmore, singing songs to himself and is rather chilly without his coast—but he is ready to fight.

For all the mischief, the host of the Garter Inn is responsible. When they meet, they meet as friends. Anne thinks that

Fenton is a fool and that Doctor Caius is no better. When she sees him, she is unhappy: "Alas! I had rather be set quick i'th earth, and bowl'd to death with turnips" (III,iv,84-5).

However, in a merry comedy, she is to be the Fairy Queen. Her father wants Slender to spirit her away and marry her at Eton, while her mother wants Doctor Caius to take her away to the deanery, and Fenton intends to spirit his Anne away and marry her at the church. But much of the fun arises from the misled Page, who thinks that his daughter is dressed in white; Anne's mother has told the doctor that she will be dressed in green. So Fenton, cleverer than the two, has arranged to have the postmaster's boy dress in white and another boy in green; this misleads Dr. Caius, and Fenton and Anne are safely married.

The remaining part of the comedy deals with Falstaff, who arrives at Herne's Oak about midnight to find the conspirators whispering around him in the leafy Oak. Falstaff invokes love: "O powerful love, that in some respects makes a beast man; in some other, a man beast" (V,v,4-5). But he is ready to embrace the two wives of Windsor. He is punished by the children, dressed as fairies:

> Pinch him, fairies, mutually;
> Pinch him for his villainy. (V,v,98-99)

The lover in Falstaff vanishes, and he learns to be "sober" despite "of the teeth of all rhyme and reason" (V,v,123). "See now how wit may be made a Jack-a-Lent, when, tis upon all employment" (V,v,124-25).

Mistress Page is delighted at her daughter marrying Fenton, and she welcomes all, including Falstaff: "Good husband, let us everyone go home. And laugh o'er by a country fire" (V,v, 228-29).

The Merry Wives of Windsor is a good domestic comedy of middle-class people; it is a much-neglected comedy but full of "support of human follies and not of crimes". This is much closer to ordinary life than a play that deals with the foibles of kings and queens.

NOTES

1. H.W.Wells and H.H.Anniah Gowda, "Falstaff and the Vidhushaka" and "*Style and Structure in Shakespeare*" (New Delhi: Vikas, 1979).

9

MUCH ADO ABOUT NOTHING

Comparative studies of Eastern and Western dramatic literature can be useful. In particular, we might consider analogies between Shakespeare's plays and the masterpieces of the Sanskrit stage. The likeness between Elizabethan theatre and Indian classical drama defines the essentials of all good drama: the differences describe outstanding distinction between East and West, delineating the particularities of each. One hears such glib statements as that Kalidasa is "the Indian Shakespeare" or that Shakespeare is "the English Kalidasa"; they are not criticism, but may be considered international appreciation of courtesy, as if writers from countries substantially removed from each other should lift their hats or turbans with reciprocal bows. There is a certain amount of unperceptive criticism in the West, which has regretted that the Indian classics fail in many ways to resemble the classics of the Hellenic world. But classical Indian plays are closer to Elizabethan plays than to Greek drama. Sophocles is not close to Kalidasa, while Shakespeare is; hence the comedies of Shakespeare resemble some of our classical plays in spirit and tenor. The discipline of comparative literature explores such analogies.

Sanskrit playwrights shun tragedy, the seriousness and involvement with life that leads to the most convincing character delineation; they also avoid deep study of this particular problem. We may attribute this to Indian idealism, founded on a conception of felicity, not of logic. A Brecht or a Kafka generally touches life more to the quick than Kalidasa. It is not that Kalidasa or Harsha lacks profound conviction of evil and consequently a high interest of moral earnestness, but their works are also conceived in the silence of the heart. There is no violent purgation in a classical drama: disaster is always averted, and the play is designed to delineate eight sentiments, "Ashta Rasah". There are no flashes of psychological insight or political wisdom. For a few readers, Sanskrit works have created the somewhat stifling sensation that Nietzshe (who professed no religion, whose prescient observation that the death of God makes all weightless save that of his own concoction) declared, he felt, on entering a church. There are analogies but not influences in Shakespearean and Sanskrit drama; the analogies do not stem from common sources but from other kinds of similarities. Indian classical drama lacks the social criticism af Ibsen or Shaw—or, for that matter, of Moliere. But what it lacks in these respects is made up in aesthetic attraction and in the smooth transition from seriousness to comic situations which transfer the burden to the operation of fate, or *Karma*, or other philosophies of life. Hence the desire is to obtain spiritual harmony.

Kalidasa's *Shakuntala* and Shakespeare's *Much Ado About Nothing* share scenes of repudiation of a deeply loved woman. In *Shakuntala* the action is set in the threatening world of a repudiated newly married wife; and in the case of *Much Ado*, of a falsely accused maiden. In both, seriousness is transformed into the comic. While the content of the plays treats of emotions, *Shakuntala* is the more philosophical. Both illuminate a distinct facet in the nature of love: *Shakuntala* is an apologia for marriage, and *Much Ado About Nothing* is an apologia for reconciliation.

Courtship is, happily, an episode in life and not life's general rule. Although it proves intensely serious for those engaged in it and has importance in the social structure, it is secondary to more enduring features of love. Lovers, as Shakespeare reminds us, are most foolish of mortals. But love is treated in its deeper and more serious significances by both Kalidasa and Shakespeare (unlike the Japanese and the Chinese, who deal primarily not with courtship or romantic love but with marriage and the family), pleasure, violence, beauty, and devotional, erotic and ethical, personal and supernatural. In the plays under consideration, love is chastened by sufferance: "Joy could not show itself modest enough without a badge of bitterness". The heroines of both are freed from blemish and join their husbands; they illustrate themes of new life and innocence.

Although the treatment of love in Sanskrit drama enjoys

a special profoundity, this quality has not always been discerned, as some Sanskrit plays are erotic, frivolous, or melodramatic.

It is possible to interpret *Shakuntala* in a number of ways. The King who wanders into Kanva's hermitage is without an heir. On his seeing Shakuntala, he says in an aside:

Can this be Shakuntala, Kanva's daughter?
The reverned Kanva then is much mistaken
In ordering her to wear a dress of bark. (I, ii)

He falls in love with her at first sight, and it is like deep calling to the deep. She is to be the mother of an heir, and with her the play moves into its focus. Anusuya and Priyamvada, the companions of Shakuntala, romanticise the stage as do Shakespeare's women.

In *Much Ado* Claudio, who is not a prince like Dushyanta, falls in love with Hero, daughter of Leonato of Messina. Modern performances (including the Royal Shakespeare Company production of 1982) romanticise the Hero-Claudio relationship by means of stage business not warranted by the text and end by making Claudio appear perfect. But he is young, and his emotions control his reason. He wants to marry Hero because of her looks: hence Don Perdo's interference. His marriage is to bring him prosperity, even if he does not look for a "lady richly left". Claudio makes a preliminary enquiry:

Hath Leonato any son, my lord?
Don Pedro's —No child but Hero, she's his only
heir. (I,i,263-264)

In Shakespeare's play the "heir-concept" is not strong, but in Kalidasa's play a strong and unmistakable inference is that the prime reason for the union of the lovers is to secure through an heir the continuity of the dynasty. The plot deals with the obstruction to this goal, a phenomenon which must later be overcome, as in *Much Ado*. But unlike in Shakespeare, Kanva is not available when Dushyanta and Shakuntala fall in love and marry according to the rules of Gandharva-Vivah;

i.e., private or secret marriage later approved of by the parents. Early in Act IV we learn from Anusuya about the curse of Durvasa, to whose call she has not responded, being deeply obsessed with the departure of her husband. Even Anusuya is affected, she feels premonition. The evil spell, the curse of Durvasa, makes Dushyanta forget that he has effected the union. When he sees her, he is surprised:

> I have no recollection
> Of marrying this woman, and how can I
> Accept her now, when she is clearly pregnant.
> And so be guilty of adultery. (V,25-26)

This comes as a bolt from the blue: there is a torture in the heart of innocent Shakuntala. In great distress she says;

> When love like his has undergone such change,
> What is the use of forcing recollection? (V,24-25)

But she is determined, like a woman wronged in love, to prove her innocence; especially she recalls the happy moments he spent with her, the incident of the deer not drinking water from his hand but from the hand of one "who has the same scent as himself"

> My lord:—But such a manner of address
> Is now unwanted.—King of Puru's race.
> Since once when in the hermitage you made
> Promises and signs of high affection.
> To me, who loved you freely, is it right
> Now to reject me with such cruel words? (V,27-33)

Dushyanta calls her a liar. She is repudiated even as Hero: both are treated with cruelty. The reader's sense of propriety and decorum is outraged: the violence of the King's language (as intense as Claudio's in the Church scene) gives the reader or spectator a painful shock. Shakuntala is in conflict with a man of power and personality. We must take the feel of these various episodes carefully in order to appreciate the individual experiences offered by both the plays. There is a stir of conflicting emotion in the heart of Shakuntala, who bears the heir of Puru's race in her womb. Her own people also find fault with her. Gautami says that "this has been alone your private choice". A virtuous woman is suspected, and it is a difficult predicament for Shakuntala who has grown up unexposed to dangers. Tragedy is diminished by her rescue. The outlook of the playwrights differs: one averts tragedy and the other delights in it. But the atmosphere of seriousness continues, unlike in *Much Ado*. When the evil is lifted, the wedding ring is discovered. The King becomes repentant, and his desolate mood dawned upon him until in the final act (by what in reality is fate but appears as an accident) to meet both his wife and son in Maricha's hermitage. The repudiated heroine is the queen and the mother of the heir. The King has matured through suffering, and the queen learns that the engrossing burden of passion is injurious to social conduct: "Gods approve of the depth and not the tumult of the soul". In Kalidasa's view, love born of passion reaches fruition in the triangular relation of wife, husband, and child, with love being exchanged on virtually equal terms between them. In the classical theatre, both God and humans participate in the drama.

The road from Kalidasa to Shakespeare seems short, but Kalidasa is different from Shakespeare, as an artist he in *Much Ado* seems to establish equality between the sexes in a sophisticated spirit of challenge and debate. Much of the play is in prose and given to the "competitive vitality" (Rossiter) of Beatrice and Benedick, but the major part is the manoeuvring, in which Hero is repudiated and later saved.

Unlike *Shakuntala*, *Much Ado* is complicated: the two major plots involove Claudio and Hero and Benedick and Beatrice—the former serious, the latter comic. There is also the auxiliary plot of Dogberry and Verges. Claudio, who has been called a "Pitiful fellow" by Swinburne, a "hateful young cub" by Rider, and "the last amiable lover in Shakespeare" by Harbage, is described as "noble" by Beatrice. Gaiety and non-responsibility dominate the early scenes. The world of *Much Ado* is light, with only a little dark shadow to relate it to everyday reality. As Yeats said of one of his poems, "I made it out of a mouthful of air"; so could it he said of this comedy. Hence Coleridge thought *Much Ado* was an illustration of his "fourth distinguishing characteristic" of Shakespeare, in accordance with which the interest in the plot is always, in fact, on account of the characters, not vice-versa. The plot merely provides a canvas. "Take away from *Much Ado*...all that which is not indispensable to the plot, either as having little to do with it, or, at best, like Dogberry and his comrades forced into the service, when any other less ingeniously absurd watchmen and night-constables would have answered the mere necessities of the action—take away Benedick, Beatrice, Dogberry, and the reaction of the former on the character of Hero—and what remains?" Coleridge seems to be unduly harsh on this play, written mostly in prose but continues along "the......road of 'blank verse' at dramatic parts as in the earlier comedies it communicates a lightness of heart, seriousness of blame in matters of life: it is a play of sunshine and joy"[1].

> Forbid the sun to enter; like favourites,
> Made proud by princes, that advance their pride
> Against that power that bred it. (III,i,9-11)

It is a well-constructed play in which the plots run in tandem, in which harmonisation of plots, so variously derived, is effected in Act IV.

The story of blemish attached to the heroine is taken from Bendello's *Nayelli* (No.XXII), translated into French by Belleforest in *Histories Tragiques*. The story is used by Ariosto in *Orlando Furioso* (Canto V), and a variation of the story is in Spenser's *Faerie Queen*. It was a popular story during the time of Shakespeare; and post-Coleridgeans have seen merit in the play. Unlike in *Shakuntala*, there are some problems in the construction. The trouble starts from Don John who, "rich in displeasure", wants to cross the marriage between Count Claudio and Hero; the crossing is "medicinable" to him. He uses Borachio, in love with Margaret, the waiting gentlewoman of Hero, to kill Leonato and he goes about his job with great dexterity. But Hero is aware of the implications of blame; "How much an ill word may empoison living" (III,i,84). The news of her alleged disloyalty is slowly spread. Don John talks of it, and Claudio declares, "Where I should wed, there I shall shame her" (III,ii,114). The whole game is worked up in the Church scene (IV,i), just as Shakuntala is dishonoured in a Court scene. Borachio, who makes up the tale, says, "I have to-night wooed Margaret, the Lady Hero's gentlewoman, by the name of Hero; she leans me out at her mistress' chamber-window, bids me a thousand times good night—I tell this tale villely; I should first tell thee how the Prince, Claudio, planted and placed and possessed my master, Don John, saw afar off in the orchard this amiable encounter" (III,iii,135-146). One does not know how she came to occupy Hero's room. This is all planned to send Hero home again without a husband and is characterised by the Second Watchman as "the most dangerous piece of lechery that ever was known in the Commonwealth" (III,iii,154-55).

But neither Claudio nor Don Pedro is brought in here, either to overlook or overhear the scene, as Shakespeare was to show us Troilus and Ulysses eavesdropping on Cressida and Diomede. This would have given away the game. Probably Shakespeare wants to make the church scene effective by the discrimination of Claudio. The scene, like the court scene in *Shakuntala*, is agonising to all concerned. In the classical play Shakuntala dominates more. But we don't know much about Hero. But we all feel sorrow at the savage denial of marriage, coming soon after her being ready for the church.

> She's but the sign and semblance of her honour,
> Behold! how like a maid she blushes here.
> O what authority and show of truth
> Can cunning son cover itself withal!
> Would you not, swear,
> All you that see her, that she were a maid,
> By these exterior shows? (IV,i,38-42)

The two edifices collapse when Hero "dies" and Shakuntala "disappears". In both cases, a woman's honour is the central theme. The Claudio-Hero crisis resembles the Dushyanta-Shakuntala crisis. Claudio, like Dushyanta, is epithetical; they are fierce young egotists, but there is a difference: Claudio claims to have details of Hero's misconduct, while Dushyanta suffers from loss of memory. Kanva and King Leonato are filled with grief. Leonato says :

O' she is fall'n
Into a pit of ink, that the wide sea
Hath drops too few to wash her clean again,
And salt too little which may season give
To her foul tainted flesh. (IV,i,140-45)

This passage's significant metaphors ("wide sea", "tainted flesh") take the play close to the great tragedies.

When, in *Shakuntala*, Gautami reminds his daughter of her occular evidence (i.e., the ring) Shakuntala looks for it and discovers that she has lost it. The King's answer is: "This is the easy sophistry of woman." But both situations are not devoid of penetrating humanity. Friar Francis tries to save the situation from "slander to remorse", and Hero declares her innocence. Both pairs are torn apart by a misunderstanding that has begun to shatter the comic atmosphere. Hence Hero has to "die to live". The wisdom of the priest works on Leonato. At this point, Beatrice and Benedick take over. Beatrice, who is kin to Portia, wants Benedick to "kill Claudio".

The tragic scenes of the repudiation of Hero and Shakuntala and their immediate consequences form the centre of both plays. But in *Much Ado* there are several sub-plots. Leonato is occupied with his own grief. Borachio and Conrade are bound for their offences (false report, speaking untruth, slandering, and belying a lady), Borachio explaining how he courted Margaret in Hero's garment. When the truth is out, Claudio, like Dushyanta, repents:

Sweet Hero now thy images doth appear
In the rare semblance that I loved it first. (V,i,238-39)

Soon, anticipating the statue scene in *The Winter's Tale*, Leonato will say:

My brother hath a daughter,
Almost the copy of my child that's dead,
And she alone is heir to both of us.

Give her the right you should have giv'n her cousin,
And so dies my revenge. (V,i,276-79)

Claudio, invited to see "One Hero died defil'd but I do live", readily agrees:

Give me your hand before this holy friar
I am your husband if you like of me. (V,iv,58-59)

This is the theme of resurrection to which Shakespeare returns in *The Winter's Tale* and *Pericles.* While both Dushyanta and Claudio repent, their methods of repentance vary. In the Sanskrit, repentance is arduous and full of anguish. Maricha's *ashrama,* where he meets Shakuntala, is sacred; it recalls the words of Emerson in urging that a forest might be equivalent to a church. It was in "forests of suspicious trees with fragrant air to nurse their vital powers" (p. 101) that Shakuntala and Dushyanta are re-united through their son. By contrast, in Messina, Benedick says:

Let's have a dance are we are married, that we may lighten our own heart and our wives, heels. (V,iv,116-19)

The Claudio-Hero story intertwines with the stories of Dogberry and Verges, which lighten and even tighten the drama. The love story of Beatrice and Benedick enlivens the atmosphere; it begins early in the play and moves close to the Hero-Claudio plot. When Claudio denounces Hero, Benedick declares his love for Beatrice[2]. He metamorphoses from being an intimate gossip to tongue-tied suitor and icy-challenger:

A man loves the meat in his youth that he cannot
endure in his age. Shall quips and sentences and these
paper bullets of the brain awe a man from the career of
his human? No; the world must be peopled. When I said
I would die a bachelor, I did not think I should live
till I were married. (II,ii,218-23).

Benedick and Beatrice are cast in the comic mould; they

(together with Don Pedro, Borachio, Dogberry, and the Sexton) demonstrate an affirmation of belief in the power of comedy, love, and romance. Don John, the author of all mischief, is given "brave punishment", which adds to the gaiety of the wedding festivities. The play, like *Shakuntala*, ends in dance and music; it is evocative of thorough down-to-earth images.

The final movement in *Shakuntala* begins with Dushyanta's remorse, his search, and his accidental meeting with his wife. Through his son, love is fruitful not only in aesthetic terms or in those of a narrower emotional dynamics but through the ideal of the family. It signifies the fertility of both body and soul, the principles of growth, the sun-like warmth under which the noblest properties of human life attain their fullness. The sage Kasyappa, who acts as a benevolent mediator, tells Dushyanta that the boy will be the emperor of the world: "My son, your child and wife at last restored,/Fly Indra's chariot to your capital".

In *Much Ado* the finale comes at the "Hero's taunt" and a fine lyric sung by Don Pedro. The new life begins with the images of sunrise and morning. At the home of Leonato the happy couple meet:

Claudio : Give me your hand; before this holy friar,
I am your husband if you like of me.
Hero : And when I lived I was your other wife;[Unmasks]
And when you loved you were my other husband.
(V,iv,58-61)

Just as Dushyanta's curse ends with the recognition of the ring, Don John's slander is cancelled. The plays conclude with the affirmation that evil cannnot destroy lives of devotion and love. The art of Kalidasa and Shakespeare is essentially poetic; it affirms that evil does not last long and that love and faith will triumph.

NOTES

1. H. Krabbs. "Elements in Shakespeare's Construction" read at

International Shakespeare Conference, Stratford-upon-Avon, 1978.

2. In August 1982 at the Royal Shakespeare Company production of *Much Ado* at Stratford-upon-Avon, Derek Jacobi's Benedick was sheer joy. Act II, in which he learns of Beatrice's "love" for him, was brilliantly conceived, with a fine running-gig involving his page. "The world must be peopled" drew loud laughter and applause.

10

AS YOU LIKE IT

As You Like It is a single peak, but it is the most elaborate in construction among the pure comedies, although according to some scholars it is challenged by *Cymbeline*.

The Little Clay Cart, like most of Shakespeare's plays, has two plots—a major and a minor action. *As You Like It*, has at least six or seven. *The Little Clay Cart*, historically speaking, comes extremely close to being two plays, as read today. The title comes from an incident in Act VI, where Rohasen Charudatta's son, insists on having a golden toy cart from his father, now in poverty. Vasanthasena, his mother, tries to pacify him by piling her ornaments into the clay cart. The ornaments left by her are used as evidence against Charudatta. There are also other big carts: when they are accidentally interchanged, Vasanthasena rides the wrong one (belonging to Sakara). Aryaka, who has escaped from prison, hides in Charudatta's cart and thus plays his part in converting the "tragic" into the comic. The play is in ten acts, technically describad as *Prakarna*, and these give a lot of scope for the development of conflict, both tragic and comic. There are frequently two or more groups of characters who occupy the stage, imagined as invisible to each other but in closer sight of the audience. Although the cast is not limited, a considerable stage would be required to hold them all. Musicians (about a dozen in number) originally filled the back wall. As in Shakespeare, there is no curtain between stage and audience—the only curtain (to cover the two doors) is pushed aside as the actors enter. Sometimes dramas are used for ceremonial processions. Sanskrit plays are commonly provided with little scope for the individual acts. These acts are like the movements in the symphony and the sonata.

As You Like It and *The Little Clay Cart* are painted on a vast canvas. The Rosalind story and the story of Charudatta are like the trunk of a tree : the other features are the branches, and the branches extend in very dissimilar extent and direction. The condition is largely evidenced by distinctions in characterisation. "The story of an old man and his three sons" holds the dramatic mood. In seeing analogues between two plays of different civilizations, I.A. Richards's remark about the interpretation of poetry helps us. He says, "Whatever accounts are offered to the reader must leave him in a very deep sense free to choose, though they may supply wherewithal for exercise of choice." This, he added, "is not any general licence to readers to differ as they please. For this deep freedom in reading is made possible only by the widest surface conformities; for it is through surfaces...that we have to attempt to go deeper".[1]

It is possible to see parallel surfaces, techniques, or analogues between the two plays: they deal with the theme of idealisation of love, poverty, and the fool and the *Vidhushaka*, and the heroic conflict between the old and the new. Each play has its own typical blank verse, rhymed couplets, prose, but instead of courtly intrigues, we have political intrigues in another theme well-known in courtly romance. The love of a courtesan for a poor, honest man beset with difficulties as the course of true love does not run smooth and has parallels with the lovers in *As You Like it*. "My brother Jaques he keeps at school, and report speaks goldenly of his profit : for my part, he keeps me rustically at home, or, to speak more properly, stays me here at home unkempt" (I,i,4-7). The story moves quickly, like the tragic story of *King Lear* and his three daughters, expressing hate and love through the Forest of Arden, where the lovers meet, wander and write poetry on the bark of trees till all the wicked characters are reformed. The first half of *The Little Clay Cart* can be described as *Charudatta in Poverty* and the second half as *Charudatta Restored to Poverty*. But both parts are related, not as a pedestal to its statue but as a tree trunk and the many branches with their surprisingly abundant foliage. Charudatta's poverty is close to the poverty of Adam, who has a significant name.

The stage of the classical drama and that of Shakespeare are close to each other. In King Sudraka's play, Palaka (a wicked king in the sub-plot) refuses to commute the death sentence of Charudatta into one of simple exile based on the recommendations of the judge who derives authority from Manu, the law-giver. The big surprise in *As You Like It* comes when the middle brother arrives with the announcement, "I am the second son of old Sir Rowland" (V,iv,149). He tells us about the villainous Duke Frederick, and the play ends with all the wicked characters transformed into the good ones and the ringing of wedding bells.

Sanskrit drama is committed to the presence of hero and heroine and they are invariably idealised, partly because the Indian aesthetics regard all art as by rights idealistic. This idealism is not so much intellectual or moral as spiritual. Another feature that links *As You Like It* to the Indian classical play is its lyricism; that is, the singing of songs further lightening to the structure. Amiens's song is well known:

> Under the greenwood tree
> Who loves to lie with me,
> And turn his merry note
> Unto the sweet bird's throat,
> Come hither, come hither, come hither.
> Here shall he see no enemy
> But winter and rough weather. (II,v,1-7)

All culminates in song and dance in the last scene, a convention that goes back in European drama as far as Aristophanes and in Indian classical drama as far as Kalidasa.

The last act of *The Little Clay Cart* is presumably weightier in aesthetic or moral terms than passages in *As You Like It*. Samsthanaka is pardoned; Charudatta says,

> The punishment that he deserves is kindness,
> The wisdom we learn from Budha, our Lord. (p. 378)

The central episodes in both the plays move one after another. Duke Senior speaks of the woods, "More free from peril than the envious court?", and pronounces, "Sweet are the uses of adversity" (II,i,12). Charudatta is poor, but his poverty is symbolic of a feature, as (in compensation) is Vasanthasena's opulence. He speaks of poverty as "the well-spring of melancholy" (I,i,7). When his friends desert him, it is a "source of endless grief". Vasanthasena (whose name means "spring") is cast in opposition to the melancholy lover. She is aggressive and enterprising.

Long speeches about the Seven Ages of Man, Lord's description of Jaques's philosophising about the deer, and Oliver's description of his own rescue by Orlando are like the incidents in the early part of *The Little Clay Cart*—the gamblers' fight; Samasthanka, once Charudatta's servant, becoming a monk, attacked by a mad elephant; and Sarvilaka, a Brahmin by birth, committing theft to get rich to love Madanika, Vasanthasena's maid. But he is a man with a conscience. He gets into Charudatta's house by making an artistic hole, stealing the ornaments, and giving them to Madanika also a courtesan. Later, he is forced to return the jewels. They tell a lie, but Vasanthasena blesses them. As husband and wife they plan a honeymoon, using a chariot lent by Vasanthasena. But as ill-luck would have it, Aryaka, the revolutionary, has been taken prisoner by the king. He is Sarvilaka's friend; he has to choose between friendship and his honeymoon. Two other characters, Maitreya and Ratnavali (who carries a message to Vasanthasena from Charudatta) are packed into Act IV. Touchstone's job is to provide entertainment; so is the job of the *Vidhushaka*, or clown's attendant, on the hero, a Brahmin who loves good eating and all physical pleasures (except, perhaps, those of sex). The witty maid, the subservient courtier, the princely buffoon, the corpulent bawd, the mother of the resplendent and generous courtesan—all these are familiar figures on the Indian stage. But there are not as many couples in *As You Like It*, where one finds Touchstone and Corin, Silvious and Phebe, Touchstone and William, and Rosalind and Orlando.

The climax is reached in artificial verse in Shakespeare:

Phebe : Good shepherd, tell this youth what 'tis to love.
Silvious : It is to be all made of sighs and tears;
And so am I for Phebe.
Phebe : And I for Ganymede.

Orlando : And I for Rosalind.
Rosalind : And I for no woman. (V,ii,79-84)

Hero and heroine, Charudatta and Vasanthasena, the generous young man prodigal of his wealth and the noble-minded haetaera, are essentially the same figures, as in any comedy. But there are, of course, distinctions and also parallels within parallels. Major Sanskrit plays are love stories of separation, divorcement, and final union. Essentially all lovers are the same: their behaviour seems uniform. The lovers' two pairs (Charudatta and Vasanthasena in the major plot and Sarvilaka and Madanika in the minor plot) move through a storm; they meet in the garden; tension relaxes, just as the Clown suggests that the true strategy of lovers is alternation between passion and reserve. It is a study in poise to be maintained between passion and reserve and between rapidly shifting incidents that reflect, indeed, the ironic Hindu conception of the universe as a conjunction of complementary forces. This may not coincide with Jaques's witty and cynical view of a world of seven ages of man. His old age is "...Sans teeth, sans eyes, sans taste, sans everything" (II,i,166). This is in complete contrast to King Sudraka's vision of life; the whole of the Ujjayini kingdom sings of the fame of Charudutta, who is described as a "kalpa-tree" (ever yielding) which, bent under its own fruit of virtue, is growing old gracefully like Adam, whose old age is a source of worry to Duke Senior, who says, "support him by the arm. Give me your hand". (II,ii,202)

Just as irony is characteristic of the golden world at the end of *As You Like It*, so it is also of the classical play. At the conclusion, everything ends happily: at the intervention of the monk and pardoning of Sakara, the clay cart (symbolic of Charudatta's poverty and asceticism) becomes the gold cart (preferred by his son). Aryka becomes the king, and Sarvilaka sums up the entire play like the chorus in a Greek drama. He says :

Vasanthasena, the king with greatest pleasure
Confers on you the noble title wife. (p. 317)

The golden word is thus described:

May cows for ever give abundant milk,
May earth for ever bring forth its ample yields. (p. 319)

The Rosalind and Orlando story, although not very close to that of Vasanthasena and Charudatta, moves in the Forest of Arden. It is a different world, where people "live like the old Robin Hood of England". (I,i,110)

As in Sudraka, the moral, ethical element is stressed. That is, life in the forest is virtually life in an earthly paradise; that in the courtly and urbane world is represented as degenerate. The love scenes suggest youth. But artful contrasts to this are the scenes with Adam, figurative of old age. This image, highly idealistic, is also part of the classical tradition of the venerable in pastoral poetry.

In the golden world of the Forest of Arden, mundane laws are suspended and the wicked become good. The Forest, like Pushpakaranda garden in *The Little Clay Cart,* is important; it is like a character, yet the forest is less glamorous than the Pushpakaranda, where the lovers meet. The shepherd and shepherdesses who enrich the pastoral background are contrasted with the lovers of the main plot. Rosalind and Orlando are full of good sense and prosaically realistic, while Phebe and Silvius are poetically sensitive. Audrey, who does not know what poetical is, thinks "lovers are given to poetry" (III,iii,16). These characters use literary phrases but have plenty of common sense. A mixture of phrases and good sense is important in the play. The banished Duke Senior feels "the penalty of Adam"; "The reason's difference" "Finds tongues in trees, books in the running brook. Sermons in stones, and good in everything" (II,i,16-17). Phebe's literary allusion to Marlowe shows Shakespeare's debt to him: "Dead Shepherd, now I find thy saw of might" (III,v,81).

The Forest of Arden, like the island in *The Tempest* serves a dramatic purpose of place removed from the artificiality of life at court. The forest provides a congenial place for the lovers. The make-believe role of the lover is well played; Orlando, as lover, grows; his decision to save Oliver from lioness and snake and his reaching the position as full lover lacks verisimilitude but is interesting. The final revelations are serious: when he thinks of his brother's marriage, he says,

"O, how bitter a thing it is look into happiness through another man's eyes!" (V,ii,41).

The masque-like entrance of the god of marriage indicates the social relationship: "This Hymen peoples every town" (V,v,137).

By virtue of its many-coloured, intricate pattern, *As You Like It* is close to *The Little Clay Cart*. The flower of Shakespeare's play is in the poetry; the complexity of the colouring makes one think of the many colours of a clown's costume, of the vivacity of a hunch-backed *Vidhushaka*, or of the hues that one enjoyed so much in their varied autumn colours, each tree and sometimes each leaf having sensational variety. There is a desire to create the sentiment of spiritual equilibrium that leads to an elaborate structure of balance and counter-balance and a singularly firm aesthetic construction.

The Little Clay Cart is bewilderingly rich: it has lyrical expression, theatrical symbol and metaphor, soliloquy, off-stage voices, evocation of imagined agents and scenes. Its large cast of characters derives from many strata of society. *As You Like It* begins on the usurpation of property by a wicked brother; in *Clay Cart* it is the overthrow of a usurper to the throne. Like Shakespeare's comedy, it concerns everyday life; it abounds in shrewd observation and perception on politics, religion, and society. There are two major divisions: many early passages exhibit wit and comedy rather than exalted poetry: later parody stands side by side with eulogy and prayer. Sarvilaka's housebreaking is a hilarious comedy, a travesty of Brahmanic ritual. As in Shakespeare, girls pursue boys: "Journeys end in lovers meeting" (*Twelfth Night*) (I,iv,15). Vasanthasena journeys to her lover, unmindful of a rainstorm, but it is described as a hymn to the storm god, Indra, and this goes back to our Sanskrit poetic text, *Rig Veda*. It is like Blake and Tennyson shaking hands across the ages. Vasanthasena says:

> These clouds are black as rain-drenched tamarind boughs
> All light has vanished in the blinding shower
> Anthills have crumbled in the drenching rain,
> As elephants whom arrows overpower. (p.215)

She greets her lover by striking him lightly with a bouquet and inquiring for the health of "the gambler", Samsthanaka, a former servant of Vasanthasena becomes a monk. It is a witty reference: the act refers to the poise, and the ironic Hindu conception of the universe as a conjunction for complementary forces. Vast is the culmination of the love between the hero and heroine. We soon read about Rohasena, Charudatta's son, demanding a golden toy cart, not understanding that his father's poverty cannot afford it. Act VI deals with political situations, involving additional characters. Moonlight, as in Shakspeare, is conducive to lovers, and Sarvalika is escorted home. She has wealth but longs for love. Vasanthasena is her lover. When she is criticised by her maid, Madanika, for falling in love with a poor man, "Do wanton bees fly to a mango tree/After its flowers are gone?", Vasanthasena replies, "But that, my girl,/Is the reason known as wanton". (p.153)

She returns the pearls sent to her by Charudatta, putting them in a little clay cart belonging to his son, so that he may buy a golden cart. There are descriptions of a courtesan's house that are reminiscent of the same in *Measure for Measure*: it is compared to "three heavens in one place united".

Both the hero and heroine are invariably idealized, partly because the Indian aesthetics regard all art as by right idealistic. This idealism is not so much intellectual or spiritual. A play is intended to leave its audience spiritually edified, elevated, serene—though not, perhaps, the wiser through the presentation of any particular moral or ethical problem. The purgation of tragedy is not demanded, nor is the satirical wit of an intellectual comedy presented. The hero need not be conspicuously active, but he must be spiritually admirable, even though he need not be humanly perfect and must not be a prude. The pious and poor Charudatta and the pleasure-loving Vasanthasena are typical variations on the basic theme of idealisation.

Aristotle discovered that the structure of a play is to be based on its action. But *The Little Clay Cart* is much more philosophical, fundamental, spiritual, and much subtler, than most. In Act V the lovers are brought together, and though the heroine, Vasanthasena, declares that, in the dark, she has not gratified herself with the unimpeded sight of her lover (and moreover that she hasn't as yet established the ideal relation with him), at least the physical consummation of their passion may be assumed as an important step forward in their emotional relationship.

When the play opens, Vasanthasena hurries through the streets, pursued by Samsthanaka, an unwanted suitor of the courtesan whose first halfname means "spring". She takes refuge in the house of the hero, a poor honest Brahmin whom she had met at the Kamer's Temple Garden. She is in love with Charudatta. Vita, a libertine and Samsthanaka's companion, describes her:

> A courtesan keeps an open house for youth;
> She blooms for all men, like a roadside flower.
> (p.136)

But she is no ordinary courtesan; she is the one who has values, and Samsthanaka admires her. Her status puts her in a position to love kings and brahmins; she is attracted to Charudatta, who is described as "noble" and "a treasure-house of righteousness" (p.143). He is poor and has no prestige and experience. He is aware of the situation and muses:

> But since my wealth has passed from my control
> My love for her is like a coward's sage
> Powerless to issue from my tortured soul. (p.147)

His poverty is symbolic of a more general conception of privation and gives him a distinguishing feature just as (in compensation) does Vasanthasena's opulence. She is, like Rosalind, more aggressive and enterprising than her melancholy lover. His melancholy is different from that of Jaques. The reckless and acquisitive gambler, the *Vidhushaka*, or clown, attendant on the hero, being a brahmin, is a sensualist and non-vivant. In what may be termed a sub-plot, Sarvilaka, a brahmin by birth, commits theft and wants to placate Madanika, Vasanthasena's maid. He needs money for making love, and is prepared to do anything to obtain it, but his conscience bites him. He is a figure fit to be in Shaw, while Madanika is reminiscent of Maria in *Twelfth Night*. The servants in *The Little Clay Cart* are clever, not reduced to indignity; Sthavaraka is the most valiant and honest of all.

As You Like It and *The Little Clay Cart* cannot follow precisely the same pattern, although both are idealized mythologically. One is more synthetic, a story of city life and manners in which wicked men transformed into good in the forest; the other has political overtones and both have humorous and serious scenes.

In Act VIII of *The Little Clay Cart* the conflict is between the noble and the wicked, Vasanthasena and Samsthanaka (brother-in-law) of the King and a monument of villainy who wants to kill her. The scene is reminiscent of Desdemona's strength in facing her angry and unreasonable husband. She has apparently died, loving Charudatta, but her resurrection is in Act VIII. She raises her arm from a pile of fallen leaves and this constitutes a singularly lovely and dramatic symbol. The last act is spectacular; it has pageant, movement, and a poetical proclamation of Charudatta's execution announced four times by the executioners and imagined as heard in the four sections of the city. The execution is to take place at the South Gate, and Charudatta speaks several stanzas at intervals, keeping pace with the relentless march to the southern cemetery. The entire act constitutes a carefully contrived montage. It is interrupted by the pleas of Rohasena, Charudatta's son, and Sthavaraka with his plea for Charudatta's liberation, thwarted surprisingly by Smasthanaka. Guha, the executioner, says:

My father, when he was dying,
Said to me, "My son, my lusty son,
When your turn comes to execute a man,
Be sure that you do nothing hurrriedly" (p.306)

Two abortive attempts are made to halt the ceremonial march. Ultimately, a kind of *deus exmachina* (as in *As You Like It*) is the appearance of Vasanthasena, who has been supposed dead at her lover's hands, and who puts an end to the horrible proceedings. The red robe worn to execution becomes the marriage robe worn by Charudatta when Vasanthasena is elevated by Aryaka, who has succeeded Palaka and makes Charudatta his minister. The lovers become husband and wife in the changed social circumstances.

Misfortunes come in bundles: but they are all overcome. The comic muse handled by King Sudraka and Shakespeare wears different robes; but the essentials are the same. There are rituals, misfortunes, attacks on injustice, conversions of the good into the bad. There are solemnity and heavily stressed patterns which deliberately underline the control and order the picture they present King Sudraka's politics are a minor part. In both plays, there are passages weighed with poetic imagination and declaimed with the least suggestive of recitative; both plays achieve a triumph of plasticity, with speech ranging from the most exacting verse to the most colloquial prose idiom and acting styles evidently no less varied. The denouement unites the most diverse threads.

The Sanskrit world and the English world present images of unification and binding together; they are different, yet e ssentially both aim at harmony.

NOTES

1. I.A. Richards, *International Colloquies: Poems and Plays* (New York: Harcourt, Brace, Jovanovich, 1971).
2. For *The Little Clay Cart* & *Shakuntala* vide *Classical Triptych*, H. W. Wells, The Literary Press, Mysore.

11

TWELFTH NIGHT; OR, WHAT YOU WILL

It is an easy transition from *As You Like It* to *Twelfth Night*, but the latter is a play of fine confusion; deception and disguise continue. It is based on an Italian play, *Gl'Ingannati* (The Deceived One's) (1531), a comedy of mistaken identity. *As You Like It* has the freedom of the forest, while *Twelfth Night* takes place in the houses and the formal gardens of the city of Illyria and the sea-coast near it. *As You Like It* has its four pairs of lovers who move in the world of friendly courtship; in *Twelfth Night* the world of romance is of unrequited love and unreliable messengers. The playwright emphasises the pairs of lovers, a theme that appeared in *Love's Labour's Lost*. The theme of love requires different directives in plays; it has no fixed law, as in the classical comedies. The device of the disguise of the girl as a page wooing on her master's behalf is found also in *The Two Gentlemen of Verona*: the disguised Julia in the service of her false lover, Proteus. The sub-plot, involving Sir Toby, Fabian, Maria, and Feste, resembles Adriana, Luciana, the Courtesan, and Pinch with Antipholous of Ephesus, whom the other four really think possessed by the devil (*The Comedy of Errors*, IV, iv). Hence, as in other comedies, there is a persistent development of the classical irony, *odi et amor* ;

> I hate and love—ask why—I can't explain;
> I feel it's so, and feel it racking pain.

These words of Catullus could be used by innumerable playwrights in world literature. Lovers hate and love each other; Othello and Desdemona are a classic instance. But *Twelfth Night* is a mingling of farce and romance. It may not exhibit a just picture of life, but it is an enjoyable play. Gaiety and Pathos alternate, and on both the playwright has his heart.

This brings the play close to *The Little Clay Cart.*

When the play was performed on Christmas Day, 1602, by the Middle Temple, John Manningham, a spectator, said that it was "much like the *Comedy of Errors* or *Manechmi* in Plautus, but most like and nearer to that in Italian called *Ingannati*. A good practice in it to make the Steward believe his Lady Widdows was in love with him, by counterfeiting a letter as from his lady in general terms, telling him what she liked best in him, and prescribing his gesture in smiling, his apparel, etc., and when he came to practice, making him believe they took him to be mad".

This emphasis on Malvolio, the steward to the widow Olivia, is interesting. The Malvolio plot has resemblance to the tale of Apolonius and Silla as documented by Barnabe Riche in his *Fane to Militarie Profession.* But the story is far different from that of Shakespeare, and the plot is necessary for the affirmation of cheer and melancholy.

Twelfth Night is loaded with many plots, even as *The Little Clay Cart* is. The plot-complicative seems to be strength of this elusive comedy. In the use of verse and prose Shakespeare has made a strict division—prose is used by comic characters for producing naturalistic effects, and poetry is used by formal, romantic characters placed high in life. This strict division was not followed in *As You Like It*, which is laid in the forest. Whatever may be the pattern of verse and prose, one enjoys the comic muse, which stems from the music of the play, and the brilliance of Viola disguised as Cesario. One loves Viola when she is found among clowns and one likes Malvolio when he plays the role of a lover even when they are out of their depth. We move between two houses—Orsino's and Olivia's —and both are conducive to fun and frolic. Events move according to providential workings of the tale. Self-deception and alienation dominate the play. The very opening lines of the Duke Orsino strike a note in keeping with the gay charm of Illyria:

> If music be the food of love, play on,
> Give me excess of it, that, surfeiting,
> The appetite may sticken, and so die. (I,i,1-3)

Although Shakespeare treats love more as an affair of the imagination than of the heart, the play deals with the absurdities of many situations in love, which forms the basis of comedies all over the world. *Twelfth Night* is a comedy of joy set on the borders of human trivality and infectious love. The Duke loves Olivia, "who purged the air of pestilence", but she in turn pays the debt of love to a dead brother. All this suggests the remoteness of the comedy from the actual world, but it soon steps into it. The playwright follows the conventions of love of the courtly world, Olivia's vow to live like a cloistress for seven years does not make the Duke give up hope. He knows that one who cares for a brother will also care for a lover:

> O, she that hath a heart of that fine frame
> To pay this debt of love but to a brother,
> How will she love when the rich golden shaft
> Hath killed the flock of all affections else
> That live in her; when liver, brain, and heart,
> These sovereign thrones, are supplied and filled,
> Her sweet perfections, with one self king. (I,i,33-39)

He loves Olivia; he is excited; "Love-thoughts lie rich when canopied with bow'rs" (I,i,41). When Maria announces a young gentleman desiring to speak with Olivia, her question seems to be born of disgust : "From the Count Orsino, is it?" Love, in Shakespeare, as in Kalidasa, is a very serious thing; so is marriage. From the beginning, it is clear that Olivia's mourning for her dead brother is based on sentiment and not on seriousness. She is sentimentally mourning her dead brother: Orsino's love is also sentimental. Feste tells him:

> Now, the melancholy god protect thee, and the tailor make thy doublet of changeable taffeta, for thy mind is a very opal (II, iv, 74-76)

Sentimental love needs music and a song: "That old and antique" one (II,iv, 3). The Duke's image in respect of woman sounds sentimental:

For women are as roses, whose fair flow'r
Being once displayed, doth fall that very hour.
(II, iv, 39-40)

Shakespeare puts beautiful songs into the play, but they are not always in the right place. The Clown's singing of "Come away, come away, death" (II, iv, 53) is very in-appropriate for a man experiencing "sweet pangs" of love. When Duke meets Viola in man's attire, he can identify her as a girl:

Dian's lip
Is not more smooth and rubious; thy small pipe
Is as maiden's organ, shrill and sound. (I, iv, 81-83).

All is right in a play of "What you will"; it is a play of disguise. But Viola does undertake a painful job as she herself is in love with him. This is the mischief of disguise.

We meet Olivia in a delightful conversation with the Clown. His jokes about her brother's soul being in hell are taken in good spirit. She does not appear to be a lady in mourning. Malvolio, being a puritan, objects to her ladyship taking delight "In such a barren rascal" (I,v,83), but she rebukes him and tells him, "there is no slander in an allowed fool" (I,v,88).

The conversations between Olivia and Viola are farcical, and even as artificial as the story itself. Viola, disguised as a page, speaks words as if they were taken from a play; she speaks of "casting away my speech". To the question, "Are you a comedian?", Viola's reply is, "No, my profound heart...I am not that I play" (I, v, 175-176). Her text lies in "Orsino's bosom", and she says she would be prepared to be "a willow cabin at your gate" (I, v, 254). By the time the scene nears its end, Olivia falls in love with the disguised Viola; this is another aspect of the romantic comedy worked into *As You Like It*. Olivia wants Viola again:

You come to me again.
To tell me how he takes it. (I,v,267-8)

The "outside" of Viola has attracted Olivia, who forgets that she is mourning her brother's death. This is part of the farce. She finds support in "What is decreed must be and be this so" (I, v, 297). Viola becomes the centre of the play. She is a very charming character—a very fine creation towards the end of Shakespeare's writing of comedies and looking forward to the heroines in the romances. One can fully endorse John Wain's description of Viola standing at the exit of this garden of Shakespearean comedy. "And as she sings us out, she closes the gate behind us". On receipt of the ring that Olivia sends through Malvolio, she muses on the strange but romantic relationship that develops between her and Olivia, whom she describes as "too proud" and speaks of the effects of disguise:

> Disguise, I see thou art a wickedness
> Wherein the pregnant enemy does much. (II, ii, 26-27)

She comments on the status of women:

> Alas, our frailty is the cause, not we
> For such as we are made of, such we be. (II, ii, 29-31)

In a very important soliloquy (II, ii, 16-40) she analyses her feelings, the essence of which is:

> My master loves her dearly;
> And I (poor monster) fond as much on him.
> (II, ii, 32-33)

Elsewhere, Shakespeare speaks of wife's frailty (*Merry Wives of Windsor*) (II, i, 240) and in *Hamlet's* "Frailty, thy name is woman" (I,ii,140). And Cleopatra speaks of "Frailties which before, Have shamed our sex" (V, ii, 123) and the concluding couplet in *Twelfth Night*

> O Time, thou must untangle this, not I;
> It is too hard a knot for me t'untie. (II, ii, 39-40)

This aspect of woman, more than man, occupies the mind of the playwright in his loveliest creation, whose acute predicament cannot be better explained:

As I am a man,
My state is desperate for my master's love,
As I am a woman (now alas the day!) (II, ii, 35-37)

In this early comedy, these thoughts, although they might seem to be out of place, demonstrate the inner feelings of a character in a difficult situation.

As a woman disguised as a man, Viola plays the part well; she can comment on men in general:

We men may say more, swear more ; but indeed
Our shows are more than will. (II, iv, 115-116)

Viola judges human beings better than Olivia does. She knows that the Clown is "wise enough to play the fool" (III, i, 58); she is business-like when she acts as the messenger of Orsino and quick in her dealings with Olivia. Hence E.K. Chambers writes that "with the specific of simple truth she purges the pestilence of artifice and rhetoric". But sometimes rhetoric comes fully, as in her reply to Olivia that she is servant to the Count Orsino :

And he is yours and his must needs be yours.
Your servant's servant is your servant, madam.
(III,i, 98-99)

Olivia, who was mourning, gives up her mask bit by bit to fall in love with Caesario: she wants her to "undertake another suit":

I had rather hear you to solicit that,
Than music from the spheres. (III,i,105-106)

Viola, like Rosalind, can brave any difficult situation. She tells Olivia, "I am not what I am" (III,i,139), but Olivia does not understand the strange situtation; so she reinforces : "Love sought is good, but given unsought is better" (III,i,152).

Viola blushes and is placed in a very painful situation. The playwright, by a clever device (as in *A Midsummer Night's Dream*) keeps the emotion of the lovers under control by the use of conflicts and cryptic line-by-line exchanges which emphasise the pregnant statement, "I am not what I am" or "A little thing would make me tell them how much I lack of a man" (III,iv,282-283).

The play hinges on love, in irresistible passion, as in *Shakuntala.* While in the classical play it is between the hero and heroine, in *Twelfth Night* it is more complicated: Orsino loves Olivia, Viola loves Orsino and Olivia loves disguised Viola. This forms the core of the play. But these are lovers who do not settle down: the love of Shakuntala and Dushyanta finds fulfilment in having an heir and continuing the rule of the dynasty. It is not so in the case of these lovers. At least in the romances, which come closer to classical plays, there is a fervent desire to see that the family grows. In the recognition scene, which reminds us of scenes in *Pericles* and *The Winter's Tale*, Viola is rewarded for the services rendered "so much against the mettle of your sex" (V,i,312): she shall be Orsino's mistress and his fancy's queen (V,i,317). But she cleverly plays her role of the fiction of man-to-man conversation about love and women with the Duke and Olivia.

While we are engaged in discussing the part of Viola in the play, the story of the Duke and Olivia seems to recede into the background. This seems to be the intent of the playwright, who makes the principal lovers not see each other for about three acts. Things happen quickly to the Duke, the moment Caesario comes into his life "to unfold the passion of his love" (I,v,24). The Clown's song, "Come away, come away death" (II,iv,50-65) is placed rather incongruously before the love-stricken Duke. But the "sea image", of the song "thy doublet of changeable taffeta" in the Clown's reply indicates his restlessness in love. Olivia, who gives up the facade of mourning to fall in love with Cesario, shares some of the qualities of the Duke: she is also restless before she declares her love for Cesario. When the Duke meets Olivia, he is full of affection: "Here comes the Countess: now heaven walks on earth". (V,i,91).

The revelry of the play is contributed by the members of Olivia's household; the characters live in a privileged enclave of fantasy and frivolity, a world of cakes and ale. Sir Toby Belch introduces the note of frivolity:

> What a plague means my niece to take the death of her brother thus? I am sure care's an enemy to life. (I,iii,1—2)

Maria objects to his keeping "ill hours", but this world is limited; it is the world of all. Sir Toby Belch, who has a name that speaks for itself, is a lover of drink, one who can toast his niece's health by drinking "as long as there is a passage in my throat" (I,iii,35). He can only think of Sir Andrew Aguecheek to be Olivia's lover: he is "a great eater of beef" (I,iii,74), which does harm to his wit. The brief dialogue between him and Sir Toby is delightful and adds to the comic atmosphere. He talks about his "head of hair" which "hangs like flax on a distaff" and which he has hopes "to see a housewife take thee...between her legs, and spin it off" (I,ii,91). But Sir Andrew has intellectual tastes. He delights "in masques and revels sometimes together" (I,iii,100-112). Sir Toby, who appears to be more intelligent than Sir Andrew, says "My very walk should be a jig; I would not so much as make water cut in a sink-a-pace" (I,iii,126—27). In this company of mirth and joy, Feste and Maria shine. Their meeting is indeed delightful. When Maria threatens him and tells him that his lady will hang him for being absent, his response is:

> Many a good hanging prevents a bad marriage, and for turning away, let summer bear it out. (I,18—19)

The Clown can make a joke about the soul of Olivia's brother: it is in hell and not in heaven.

Malvolio, who is evidently out of sorts in the company of Sir Toby and the others, objects to Feste's behaviour; he calls him "a barren rascal" (I, v 82). Olivia's defence is admirable: "O, you are sick of self-love...There is no slander in an allowed fool, though he do nothing but rail; nor no railing in a known discreet man, though he do nothing but rail" (I,v,87—90). Like the *Vidhushaka* of a Sanskrit play, he has plenty of freedom, which Malvolio resents. This is the comic tradition common to both East and West. Feste is a wise fool whose definition of a drunken man is hilarious: "Like a drowned man, a fool, and a madman. One draught above heat makes him a fool, the second mads him, and a third drowns him" (I,v, 124—127).

Malvolio, a puritan, is a kill joy in a modren cliche, and full of self-love. But in the course of the play there is regeneration in the discovery of his real and nobler self. In his dealing with Viola, Malvolio asserts his position as a steward and asks "him" not to come again "unless it be to report your lord's taking of this"(II,ii,9—10). But he loves drink and toasts nicely in wine. Feste's references to Malvolio are always derogatory, and one is, "His nose is no whipstock" (II,iii,27). As a steward, Malvolio is very close to Maria, which excites jealousy in other characters. He tries to assert his authority and throws his weight about. "Do ye make an alehouse of my lady's house, that ye squeak out your coziers' catches without any mitigation or remorse of voice?" (II,iii,82—84). He dares to tell Sir Toby, Olivia's kinsman, "If you can separate yourself and your misdemeanours, you are welcome to the house. If not, and it would please you to take leave of her, she is very willing to bid you farewell" (II,iii,90—92). He becomes bossy, and an easy prey to gulling. Sir Toby attacks the puritan in Malvolio: "Dost thou think because thou art virtuous, there shall be no more cakes and ale?" (II,iii,106—107). Malvolio tells Maria, who is the cleverest of the lot, not to give means "for this uncivil rule" (II,iii,112). He offends everybody in the play. Maria knows that he is "the devil a Puritan", "a time-pleaser; an affectioned ass, that cons state without book, and utters it by great swarths" (II,iii,134—37).

Maria and Sir Toby plan to gull him; the isolated figure in Illyria imagines that the contents of the letter put in his way are true.The authors of the gulling watch Malvolio's behaviour on reading the love letter supposed to have been written by Olivia. Fabian describes him thus; "contemplation makes a rare turkey cock of him. How he jets under his advanced plumes!" (II,v, 29—30). This comes true on his seeing the letter: he becomes an expert in anagrams. M.O.A.I.—this applies to him and to nobody else. He is ready to get into yellow stockings and have cross-gartered. For a moment, he forgets that yellow is the colour disliked by Olivia. His imagination runs riot, and he is delighted and he speaks of his plans when he becomes the master of the household. He will get himself educated: "I will read politic authors". (IV,v, 148). This is to baffle a gentleman like Sir Toby, who is determined to fool him"black and blue" (II,i,10). Maria, who is behind the plot of making Malvolio "a contemplative idiot" (II,i,19), prepares her companions to watch "the trout that must be caught with tackling" (II,i,19—20). Malvolio, who is a victim of his pride and self-righteousness, truly behaves like "a rare turkey-cock". It is a very humorous scene in which he tells the audience how he will treat the other characters in Olivia's household when he becomes its master. He tells Sir Toby, "you must amend your drunkenness" (II,v, 74). Malvolio is full of his incurable self-love and hence the "sinews of (the) plot" engulf him. "If you desire the spleen and will laugh yourselves into stitches, follow one" (III,iii,65-66), says Maria, the author of the plot. She and her friends become choric characters. They know that Olivia, who has seen him follow the instructions of the letter closely, is aware that Olivia will not like his demeanour; she will strike him: "If she do, he'll smile, and take't for a great favour" (III,ii,73—74). At the supreme moment of his appearance at Olivia's court, the ridicule reaches its height. Malvolio can speak the language of a lover: "Sweet Lady?", "Lady lady", "My sweet-heart". Then Olivia dismisses him: "This is very midsummer madness" (III,iv,55). Malvolio attributes the "greatness thrust upon him" to Jove, who "is the doer of this" (II,iv,76) while he is on his way to the darkroom, and Olivia believes that he is mad. His cry from prison—"As I am a gentleman"—indicates that he is prepared to learn from life.

Malvolia, in the darkroom, leads a haunted life. It is the image of a proud man being humbled; it is part of the didacticism of the comedy. Maria has more plans for fooling Malvolio. Feste is dressed as Sir Topas and made to look "a careful man and great scholar" (III.ii,210). The dialogue between the Clown (disguised as Sir Topas) and Malvolio in the darkroom is part of the comic tradition. Sir Toby and Maria are detached spectators; under their supervision the comic muse has her full play. Malvolio says that he is laid in "hideous darkness" (IV,ii,31). He reiterates that he is not mad but that the house is dark. He throws a challenge to the Clown: "I am no more mad than you are. Make the trial of it in any constant question".

(IV,ii,46—48). Hence comes the question on the opinion of Pythagoras concerning wildfowl. But Sir Topas has respect for Malvolio's opinion on the doctrine of transmigration of souls and he turns it into a jest, and Malvolio's appeal to Sir Topas falls on deaf ears. But Maria's comment is characteristic:

Thou mightiest have done this without thy beard and gown. He sees thee not. (IV, ii, 63-64)

It shows how Malvolio is isolated. It is a symbol of his keeping distance from other characters. His talk is characterised as "vain bibble babble" (IV, ii, 94). But Clown's song, "I am gone, sir, And anon sir", (IV, iii, 118-120) does not seem to fit in. It does not add to the pathos of the situation. When the deception is explained to Malvolio, he emerges heroic in an enlightened manner. When he encounters Olivia for the last time, Malvolio is humbled, no longer self-righteous, and tells her, "Madam you have done me wrong". "Notorious wrong" (V, i, 321-22). "Olivia is responsive:" "Have I, Malvolio? No." (V, i, 323). When he tells her that she made him "the most notorious geck and gull ' (V, i, 344) and the whole plot is unravelled, he shouts, "I'll be revenged on the whole pack of you" (V, i, 379). Malvolio and Sebastian are cast as mirror opposites. Malvolio becomes the victim of conventional deception, and Sebastian (earlier presented with Olivia's love) wonders whether it is fantastic illusion. Malvolio insists that he is not mad, which is clear from his soliloquy containing, "That this may be some error, but no madness". (IV, iii, 10). His words are similar to those of Malvolio, who sets his heart on Olivia and sets his clue on the wing of fantasy, which carry him away and then suddenly he plummets down to earth again. He no longer smiles meaninglessly. Olvia is aware that "He hath been most notoriously abuse'd". The comic plot flourishes on false images: Maria's letter, Feste as Sir Topas, Malvolio's dress as a lover, and the disguise of Sebastian as Viola.

The reunion of the twins, kept till the end of the play, forms part of an important ingredient of the comedy. Sebastian's entry helps solve Viola's predicament, which brings the action close to a miracle. The stage is prepared with all the important characters reassembling, as in other plays of Shakespeare. It moves up to a cresendo as the Clown tells the Duke: "Marry, sir, lullaby to your bounty till I come again" (V, i, 40-41). Thus he vanishes, but action embodies the meeting of the twins, who have been in the roles of the lovers. But they emerge from a single personality. Viola appears as a body "betroth'd both to a maid and man" (V, i, 261), but keeps her disguise till the very end. Sebastian is cast more in a feminine mould : "My bosom is full of kindness, and I am yet so near the manners of my mother, that, upon the least occassion more, mine eyes will tell tales of me" (II, i, 35-37).

Sebastian allows himself to take the place of Viola with Olivia and he can also deal firmly with Olivia's kinsman, Sir Andrew. He is a man "who is the very devil incardinate" (V, i, 174). Viola is mistaken for the King Sebastian and the Duke exclaims on seeing "One face, one voice, one habit and two persons:" (V, i, 208). This role of Cesario adds to the magic of the play caused by the disguise of Viola, who ultimately submits to time : "O, Time, thou must untangle this, not I". Olivia also knows that "What is decreed must be; and this be so!" Fate brings the twins together and solves their problems. The meeting of Orsino and Viola is like the meeting of Dushyanta and Shakuntala in Kalidasa's play. Although the Shakespeare pairs have not suffered like Kalidasa's, there were hindrances in the path of love. The pairing of lovers is cleverly done, and it is the symbol of the single desire of human beings to meet each other in love or "an exposure of the reviality of human desire". But it seems the right conclusion for a festive comedy which deals with love. The Duke, in a pleasant mood tells Viola, "Let me see thee in thy woman's weeds (V, i, 269).

She is to be the Duke's "mistress and his fancy's queen". (V, i, 377). The marriage does not seem to lead to the continuation of the family, as in *As You Like It*; or as in *Shakuntala*. The last moods of the play are festive, jovial; they denote Shakespearean gift for the magically expressed Clown's song :

A great while ago the world begun,

With hey, ho the wind and the rain;
But that's all one, our play is done,
And we'll strive to please you every day. (V, i, 394-97)

However, the play itself hints at satiety and the desire to get back to normal.

12

ALL'S WELL THAT ENDS WELL

This play, first printed in the Folio of 1623, is ironically titled, for the theme is rather sad for a comedy set in France and Italy and based on Boccaccio's *Decameron*. (It is the ninth story told on the third day, illustrating the theme "Virtue is the true nobility").

It is a play not much discussed, but Helena was praised by Coleridge and Bernard Shaw considered her his favourite heroine, as she took the initiative in wooing and winning her man. Shakespeare always took great care in naming his plays. The title reminds one of *As You Like It*, *Much Ado About Nothing* and *Twelfth Night*, Or *What You Will*—titles that suggest that the playwright is not very serious about the content: but this view is belied.

However, *All's Well* is normally considered with *Troilus and Cressida* and *Measure for Measure* as a problem comedy, one that does not fall into the category of tragedy and yet is too serious and analytic to fit the commonly accepted conception of comedy. As Dowden has pointed out, it is possible to apply the biographical criticism that Shakespeare had ceased to be able to smile genially, and had either to be ironical or else to take a deep passionate, tragical view of life, and that this spoilt him, at the time, as a writer of comedy. Dover Wilson is of the view that the three plays are an expression of pessimism and despair and exhibit a "note of disillusionment and cynicism", an outlook that is cheerless and often unwholesome. C.J. Sisson, in *The Mythical Sorrows of Shakespeare*, attacked the romantic notion that the plays were the works of a desperate man; F S. Boas saw the societies of the plays as ripe and rotten; W.W. Lawrence discerned the fallacy in the autobiographical approach and looked at the plays as demonstrating a preplexing and distressing complication in the human mind. One need not be afraid of the problems of the "problem" plays, as life is full of problems and is also unpredictable, and drama mirrors life. A play like *Mrichakatika* has more problems than the span of a single man's life would throw up. But it is the the duty of a critic to study the plays and examine them as theatre.

All's Well and *Measure for Measure* share certain common elements : the trick of the substituted bed, test of chastity, disguise, Italian origins, and long fifth acts. But *Measure for Measure* is a very austere play, illustrating the highly serious Christian doctrine of chastity; and *All's Well* is really strategy with little emphasis on human nature—an unloved woman winning her husband through a trick and in this process the woman and the mother-in-law playing a major role. For Helena it is really *Love's Labour's Won*. It is the women who dominate, as in the early comedies.

Shakespeare has invented characters, particularly the Countess of Rossillion, the mother of Bertram, while Parolles, a follower of Bertram, adds to the structure of the play and Lafew, an old lord, is a lively addition. The play has not had extensive performance, perhaps the modern mind is repelled by the plot; the wooing is on the female foot. Helena, a gentlewoman to the Countess and the orphaned daughter of a famous doctor whom the Countess has welcomed into her household, falls in love with Bertram but cannot marry owing to class differences. Her falling in love with Bertram is like that of any other of Shakespeare's women.

> 'T was pretty, though a plague,
> To see him every hour; to sit and draw
> His arched brows, his hawking eye, his curls,
> In our heart's table—heart too capable
> Of every line and trick of his sweet favour. (I,i,90—95)

She falls in love with him instinctively, and her insterest in him makes her follow him to France on the pretext of treating the ailing king.

The play opens with laboured word-play. The Countess, who is saying good-bye to her son, Bertram, on his way to the court of the King of France in the company of Lafew, says "In delivering my son from me I bury a second husband" (I,i,1–2).

Bertram is a "bright particular star", high above the social status of Helena. When he arrives at the court of France he is warmly treated by the sick King. Helena is strongly affected by his departure to France: "but now he's gone, and my idolatrous fancy/Must sanctify his relics" (I i,93–94). The Countess blesses him in rhymed couplets:

Be thou blest, Bertram, and succeed thy father
In manners, as in shape. Thy blood and virtue
Contend for empire in thee, and thy goodness
Share with thy birthright. (I,i,56 59)

Although a sad story for comedy, it has the elements of romance. Helena's love for Bertram is as intense as Juliet's for Romeo. The Countess understands "the mystery of her loneliness", and Helena admits this truth:

Then I confess
Here on my knee before high heaven and you,
That before you, and next unto high heaven,
I love your son.
My friends were poor but honest; so's my love.
Be not offiended, for it hurts not him
That he is loved of me. (I,iii,182–9)

The Countess is one of the most understanding of Shakespeare's early characters. She is sympathetic and feels like a mother to Helena. She plays a great role in the reunion of Helena and Bertram. As the plays develops, Helena tells the Countess that she would like to go to Paris to try one of her remedies on the ailing King.

There is a remedy, approved, set down,
To cure the desperate languishings where of
The king is rendered lost. (I,iii,221–23)

"The poor unlearned virgin" sets off for the French court with the Countess's blessings. Her heart's desire of seeing Bertram is fulfilled.

There is progress in his story. Helena, when she arrives at the French court, which is disturbed owing to Italian wars, timidly enters the King's room and tells him of her father who, "On's bed of death", gave her remedies:

> Of my dear father's gift stands chief in power,
> I come to tender it and my appliance,
> With all bound humbleness. (II,i,112—14).

But the King wants to die quietly because "the congregated college have concluded/That labouring art can never ransom nature" (II,i,117—18).

Helena is persuasive; she is confident that she can cure him. She appears to be a demagogue more mature than the women of other early comedies: She asserts "great floods have flown/From simple source" (II,i,140—41). She is not an imposter; she is willing to take her life on her conviction that she can cure the King. "My art is not past power, nor you past cure" (II, i, 158). Ultimately, Helena wins: "Sweet practiser, thy physic I will try," (II, i, 185) says the King.

If he is cured, Helena can have any man in the court as her husband. She is anxious:

> To choose from forth the royal blood of France,
> My low and humble name to propagate
> With any branch or image of thy state. (II,i,196—98)

Helena succeeds where the learned doctors have failed, and her success reaches Bertram's ears. Lafew observes, "they say miracles are past; and we have our philosophical persons, to make modern and familiar, things supernatural and causeless. Hence is it that we make trifles of terrors, ensconcing ourselves into seeming knowledge, when we should submit ourselves to an unknown fear." (II, iii, 1-6)

This is a very sombre note; a sense of the limited knowledge of the great unknown belongs rather to tragedy than to comedy, but throughout *All's Well That Ends Well* there is that seriousness which rightly belongs to a serious play. Helena's action demonstrates "A showing of a heavenly effect in an earthly actor." (II,iii,23-4)

Helena deserves other desserts. She is low born and has to contract a morganatic marriage. She says, "I am a simple maid" (II,ii,65), but the King is on her side: "Make your choice and see/who shuns thy love shuns all his love in me" (II,iii,72-73). Her choice of her husband is like a *swayamvara*, observed in the Eastern epics. She looks at the French lords but her choice falls on Bertram, the young Count of Rossillion. To her, "This is the man" (II,iii,187). But Bertram is not prepared to marry her, because

> She had her breeding at my father's charge.
> A poor physician's daughter my wife! Disdain
> Rather corrupt me ever! (II,iii,113-15)

The King persuades Bertram:

> Not by the title. She is young, wise, fair;
> In these to nature she's immediate heir. (II,iii,130-31)

Yet he insists that he can give her honour;

> Virtue and she
> Is her own dower; honour and wealth from me.
> (II,iii,142-43)

When arguments based on social status fail, he uses the arguments of her heart; "I cannot love her, nor will strive to do it" (II,iii,144).

The King is in an embarrassing situation; his threats and abuses do not seem to move Bertram, so Helena tries to release the King from his promise: "That you are well restored, my lord, I'm glad./Let the rest go" (II,iii,146-97). But the King is adamant and uses his authority. He decrees that the wedding shall take place that night, and he blesses them:

> Good fortune and the favour of the king
> Smile upon this contract··· (II,iii,176-77)

Although Bertram agrees to marry Helena, he is determined not to bed her. As in other plays of Shakespeare, the main character has companions to share his thoughts. Parolles, who can understand Bertram, is mean; Bertram knows that Parolles a magnificient soldier, pours out all his troubles to him.

O my Parolles, they have married me!
I'll to the Tuscan wars, and never bed her. (II,iii,265-66)

Parolles agrees with the friend's plan:

> To th'wars,
> my boy, to th' wars; (II,iii,272)

Parolles is comical, boastful, and a hanger-on of Bertram. He also makes fun of anyone who stays at home to cling to his "kicky-wicky". Bertram runs away, leaving his house and his detested wife. Parolles adds fuel to the fire: he is base and even misguiding: "A young man married is man that's marred". (II,iii.292).

Bertram considers Helena his "dog" and before deserting her, he writes a letter to his mother, Countess of Rosallion, in which he says, "I, have sent you a daughter-in-law: she hath recovered the king, and undone me. I have wedded her, not bedded her and sworn to make the 'not' eternal. Your unfortunate son, Bertram" (III,ii,20-24).

All this shows his hatred of Helena, a poor girl, but the Countess's sympathies are with Helena:

> That twenty such rude boys might tend upon
> And call her hourly mistress. (III,ii,79-81)

She characterises her son's letter as "dreadful". "When you can't get the ring upon my finger, which never shall come off, and show me a child begotten of thy body that I am father to, then call me husband: but in such a 'then' I write a 'never' (III,ii, 55-59). His letter lays down the impossible condition. But clever as she is, she tries to circumvent it. The rest of the play deals with it. Helena thinks that she has forced Bertram away from the safety of the French court and into the dangers of war, and so she decides to go on a pilgrimage, hoping that her absence will enable Bertram to return to France. The Countess is torn between her love for her son and for her daughter-in-law. The news reaches Bertram that Helena has run away. All these complications enrich the comic situation embodied on a very thin premise. At times the play borders on farce. Bertram is not without love: he is prepared to make advances to Diana, daughter to the widow who runs a lodge; and the women of Florence, who await the return of the soldiers, even they disapprove of Bertram's behaviour and his persistent love for Diana. The conversation between Diana and the disguised Helena is interesting. Diana tells Helena:

> He stole from France,
> As 'tis reported, for the king had married him
> Against his liking. (III,v,50-52).

Bertram emerges as a "young puppy": he is immature. He comes under the bad influence of Parolles, who acts as a go-between in his attempt to have an affair with the reluctant Floretine Diana. His heart and soul prove false as the play develops. All three women, Helena, Diana, and her mother, a widow who runs a lodging for pilgrims discuss Bertram and Parolles. They disapprove of Bertram's attempt to corrupt the honour of a maid.

Helena's reaction is natural : she wishes that Bertram loved his wife. But she unburdens her heart to the Countess, and a plot is hatched. Diana, who pretends to yield to Bertram, shall demand

> A ring county wears,
> That downward hath succeeded in his house
> From son to son, some four or five descents
> Since the first father wore it. This rings he holds
> In most rich choice. (III,vii,22—26)

All's Well has the strain of morality in it; Helena,who belongs to a lower rank than Bertram, has a right to love him, and hence she determines to recover him: it is for his good.

She does not want Bertram to be a sinner. Helena, like Shakespeare's other women, is clever and intelligent; she is intrinsically good, and she has cured the King of his incurable disease. She has won Bertram as a recompense for her service. Reconciliation and reunion seem always to have been uppermost in the mind of Shakespeare. These values become tangible in the Last Plays, the Romances, where romance and realism work through the younger generation to bring the older generation together. Hence, Shakespeare is in search of a device. In *All's Well* the bed-trick which brings Bertram and Helena (disguised as Diana) together, is a step towards Shakespeare's formula.

Bertram, who is burning with "the quick fire of youth", makes love to Diana. He spends the dark night with Helena, thinking that she is Diana. In this scene, Bertram is exposed as a liar, a letcher, and a hypocrite. He emerges unsucessful in all these human activities; Helena's bed-trick succeeds. It is ironic and she observes, "when I was like this maid/I found you wondrous kind" (V,iii, 308—9). Bertram loves her passionately because he firmly believes she is someone other than Helena. Ring versus chastity becomes the topic of conversation. Shakespeare, who has been musing on the value of honour in the portraits of Hotspur and Troilus, lets himself go in a situation involving Helena and Bertram: while the ring is an honour "longing to our house chastity is the jewel of Helena's house" (IV, ii,47). Conditions are fulfilled in darkneses, and they both give into each other.

The play is about exposure to human nature. Parolles is contemptible, unworthy to be Bertram's friend, a braggart who boasts about getting back his drum. The adventure of "the bringing off his drum" is a by-word for all ridiculous and blustering undertakings that a person cannot fulfil. Parolles undertakes the recovery of this drum, "Tongue, I must put you into a butterwoman's mouth —if you prattle me into these perils" (IV, v, 33-38).

The French lords play ducks and drakes with Bertram and leap upon him shouting gibberish in such lines as 'Throca movousus" and "Oscorlidilchos Valivorco". He promises to reveal everything if he is saved. He is described as a follower of Parolles, of good birth, of good breeding, but has no eye for the beauty of Helena. He is the kind of young man whom the Countess would not like to see again in her house. In a way he is important to the scheme of the play, even as Falstaff is necessary for Prince Hal. We have two young men growing up: Parolles, a coward, treacherous and deceitful; and Bertram, growing to manhood. More complications ensue: Helena's supposed death on her pilgrimage and Parolles's giving up all the military secrets and consequent betrayal of everyone. He speaks of virginity, very much as Falstaff speaks of honour. But he cannot be a Falstaff, as he inspires no affection in us. He says that "every braggart shall be found an ass" (IV,iii,313).

In the Florentine camp the two lords act as narrative, or chorus:

First Lord : Now, God delay our rebellion! As we are ourselves, what things are we!

Second Lord : Merely our own traitors. And as in the common course of all treasons, we shall see them reveal themselves, till they attain to their abhorred ends, so he that in his action contrives against his own nobility, in his proper stream o'er flows himself. (IV, II ,18-24).

The Comment is worthy of Shakespeare who insists on re-consiliation. The King forgives Bertram's offense and the story of the ring is revealed. Act V is filled with Diana's intervention; she accuses Bertram of the midnight meeting. Helena, like the Queen in *The Winter's Tale*, appears and solves all the confusion, and Bertram is doubly won. Diana, too, gets her reward. Dr. Johnson misses the spirit of the comedy when he says that Helena is "dismissed to happiness".

Other characters who help establish the structure of the play are Master Lavach, the clown, who has yet to grow to the stature of Touchstone or Feste, and the Countess, who is very much a Shakespeare creation. Lafew is honest, like old Gonzalo, and he loves and honours Helena. The play, which has the elements of farce, closes with the King's epilogue:.

The King's a beggar, now the play is done;
All is well ended ... (330-331)

NOTE

1. According to custom, the princesses would go round examining the princes and would put a garland round the neck of the one she liked best.

13

THE NARRATIVE POEMS

"In Shakespeare's poems," wrote Coleridge, "the creative powers and intellectual energy wrestle as in a war embrace. Each, in excess of strength, seems to threaten the extinction of the other. At length, in the Drama, they reconciled and fought, each with its shield before the breast of other."[1] Coleridge considers that Shakespeare started his dramatic career with his poems. There is truth in the statement, as the poems are rich and luxurious, not auster like the poetry of the romances.

"Venus and Adonis" (1580), which begins the poems, is a purple colour-patch, the "first heir" of Shakespeare, dedicated to the Earl of Southampton and presented with as much scene as any poem of Edmund Spenser. Here we have a young poet on the way to becoming famous as a poetic playwright.

"Venus and Adonis" is a narration of wanton wit, a composition of excellence in comparison with Spenser's verses. In its make-up, verse, language (colloquial and blunt and sensuous), it is highly self-conscious, in keeping with the spirit of the times. The theme of the poem is "the sensual mythological tale of the youth and the Goddess being suffused with the familiar freshness of English landscape, and the savour and the harshness of country sports"[2]

The dedication runs thus :

> I know now how I shall offend in dedicating my unpolished lines to your Lordship, nor how the world will censure me for choosing so strong a prop to support so weak a burden. Only, if your honour seem but pleased, I account myself highly praised: and vow to take advantage of all idle hours till I have honoured you with some graver labour. But if the first heir of my invention prove deformed, I shall be sorry it had so noble a godfather, and never after

so barren a land, for fear it yield me still so bad a harvest. I leave it to your Honourable survey, and your Honour to your heart's content; which I wish may always answer your own wish, and the world's hopeful expectation.

The dedication contains colloquial and even rustic and peasant expressions, and the style is easy and representative of deep feelings. The poem is for public reading, well-written in keeping with a popular theme from classical mythology, and Shakespeare must have taken it from Ovid's *The Metamorphoses* (Book X). But he works on the story and makes alterations in the relationship between Adonis and Venus. In Ovid, Adonis does not bother about Venus; in Shakespeare, Adonis is hostile to her. On the title page, *Venus* is printed small, AND ADONIS in a very large type: this directs emphasis to the youth, Venus, the goddess, as a wooer; it makes the internal struggle an attack of a higher force beyond the self. The images are disciplined: "Rose-Cheek'd Adonis" and "Sick-thoughted Venus": they speak for themselves.

O how quick is love !
The steed is stalled up.

The bolting horse is an example of the kind of animal instinct; it is set against the other animal instinct of hunting, Adonis's ruling passion. It is with great delight that one reads of the love escapades of Venus and Adonis, and the situations are strongly reminiscent of the love scenes in Eastern tales. Coleridge wrote of "an endless activity of thought with thought, thought with feeling, or with words, of feelings with feelings, and of word..." Shakespeare writes in this poem as if he were on another planet, "charming you to gaze on the movements of Venus and Adonis, as you would on the twinkling dances of the vernal butterflies".[3] It is a theme of sensuality, or erotic imagery, as is common in Sanskrit poetry :

And yet not claoy thy lips with loath'd satiety,
But rather famish them and their plenty,
Making them red, and pale. with fresh variety;

Ten kisses short as one, one long as twenty. (18-22)

These are close to the theme on *Gita Govinda* an Indian erotic poem about Krishna. The poet's description is voluptous: "And kissing speaks, with lustful language woken"; "If thou wilt chide, thy lips shall never open". Adonis lies "fasten'd in him", Shakespeare's knowledge of eroticism will put D.H. Lawrence or the author of *Kamasutra* pale into insignificance. Venus's attentions are adequate, and she handles the lovely boy as she likes. As a wooer she is human; she celebrates the "primorse bank" and other flowers which occupy the mind of the poet throughout his career.[4] Adonis is physically big; she tucks the lovely boy under an arm while she deals with the coursers's reins and then inflames the horse with a young wild-mare. She possesses "a pleading tongue" and "swelling passion". She speaks in words of a true lover: "I'll be a park, and thou shalt be my deer" (231).

Shakespeare's knowlede of horses is superb. Adonis' horse breaks lose from the tree to which he has tethered him:

Round-hoofed, short-jointed, fetlocks shag and long,
Broad breast, full eye, small head, and nostril wide,
High crest, short ears, straight legs and passing strong,
Thin mane, thick tail, broad buttock, tender hide. (295-98)

It is a magnificant picture for a painter of imagination. But Adonis responds to her love:

He wrings her nose, she strikes her on the cheeks,
He bends her fingers, holds her pulses hard. (475-76)

The poem abounds in the poet's superabounding energy; animals and landscape are used as metaphors of love. The roles are reversed; the animals also woo: horse woos his jennet.

He looks upon his love, and neighs unto her;
She answers him, as if she knew his mind
Being proud, as females are, to see him woo her,
She puts on outward strangeness, seems unkind. (307-11)

This is a pagan poem, and the images and arguments in Venus' attempted seduction of Adonis recur in the sonnets. The image "seeds spring from seeds, and the earth's increase" is common. It is celebration of ideal beauty. "Beauty hath naught to do with such foul fiends" (638).

Ultimately destruction overtakes the boar that kills Adonis. It is an image of destruction of sexual ferocity, and nuzzling Adonis with his tusk (It is taken to be a direct symbol of the plague by M.C. Bradbrook). It is a poem of beauty; but a protean transformation takes place:

> By this, the boy that by her side lay killed
> Was melted like a vapour from her sight,
> And in his blood that on the ground lay spilled,
> A purple flower sprung up, checker'd with white,
> Resembling well his pale cheeks and the blood
> Which in round drops upon their whiteness stood. (1165-70)

The conclusion resembles the story of a mystic saint, Tukaram, in an Eastern tale, who dies and out of whose grave the flowers bloom. Ovid's *The Metamorphoses* and Shakespeare's "Venus any Adonis" and some of the stories of the East seem to have a common heritage. However, "Venus and Adonis," being the first of Shakespeare's invention, demonstrates that the poet has many more creations to give us.

"The Phoenix and the Turtle" is the best of the early compositions, a sure sign of the poet's genius. The poem's outline seems to have been inspired by Chaucer's *Parliament of Fowles*,[5] also a poem about birds. The phoenix is a popular bird in Shakespeare; it is the symbol of his poetic genius. The poem is tautly constructed and devoid of digressions, unlike his other poems. The idea of the poem may also have come from *Loves Martyr*.[6] The theme of birds falling in love and dying for each other in a "manner sacrificingly" is a common theme in the stories of the East as well. But the poetic age of Shakespeare has transmuted the story borrowed from *Loves Martyr* into one of great intensity. It was the age of human idealism from which many potent, wonderful, and even transcendental personal experiences could mature, and such are the experiences behind "The Phoenix". Shakespeare's superiority lies in working in this atmosphere to create political allegory concerning Elizabeth and Essex. The aspiring poet shows his ability to use the myth of the Phoenix and the turtle to hold together in a magnificant poetic shape a poem of sixty-seven lines.

The Phoenix myth is irresistible. It is Shakespeare's favourite: "Phoenix and the turtle fled/In a mutual flame" (23-24).

The lyrical incantation of the bird falls into three divisions: an elegy on the death of the two birds, which begins by summoning the other bird to a funeral pageant; an "Antheme", which they are to sing of this mutual love; and lastly, the Antheme passes into a "Threne", the final song of their identity in love and death. Hence the three stages are lyrical; they are a wonderful addition to the poet's imaginative creation. There is variation of the metre in the quatrains in the first section and the tercets in the *threnos.* The metre depends on the word and variation of the emotions too. Threnos is a fine climb into sorrow. The lyrical quatrain which begins the poem is very evocative:

Let the bird of loudest lay,
On the sole Arabian tree
Herald sad and trumpet be,
To whose sound chaste wings obey. (1-4)

According to Wilson Knight, the bird of loudest lay is no other than the Phoenix; it celebrates the obsequies of the turtle. This is a fine interpretation, as the phoenix, a favourite symbol in Shakespeare, represents his whole corpus. Although F.T. Prince disagrees with Knight's interpretation, it is a very congenial opening and acts as a herald or the precursor to the meeting of birds. The bird is a "precursor" an "Augur", and warns "Every foul of tyrant wing" (9). There are other common birds referred to in Elizabethan literature: the swan, which sings sweetly before it dies; and the "treble-dated crow," which lives long and changes its sex at will. They form the mourning procession:

The antheme doth commence:
Love and constancy is dead. (22)

The turtle and his queen were great lovers: "Hearts remote, yet not asunder" (29).

Always, in Shakespeare, love takes precedence over reason: "Love hath reason, reason none" (47). Then the threnody in tercets is charming and thoughtful, even metaphysical, and strongly reminds one of a Donne poem:

Leaving no posterity:
'Twas not their infirmity,
It was married chastity, (59-61)

But the lines are not close to Donne. Shakespeare is rhapsodic. "The Phoenix and the Turtle" is a pointer to the austre poetry of the last plays.

"The Rape of Lucrece" is the "graver labour" that Shakespeare had promised Southampton, and it is again dedicated to him; but the tone is warmer. They are like Milton's"L'Allegro" and "Il Penseroso". But both "Venus" and "Lucrece" supplement each other.

The poem has Shakespeare's recurrent echoing and adaptation of certain Virgilian scenes born of his Roman vision, a vision which becomes progressively more critical of the values not in consonance with human instincts and needs. Such a motif is Pyrrhus, invasion of Priam's inner sanctum and his savage slaughter of the Trojan King upon an altar, recalled by Aeneas in Book II of Virgil's epic.

This sacrilegious intrusion, the climatic episode in the destruction of Troy, serves as a paradigm of Shakespeare's poem for Tarquin's violation of Lucrece.

"The love I dedicate to your Lordship is without end; whereof this pamphlet without beginning is but a superflous moiety. The warrant I have of your honourable disposition, not the worth of my untutored lines, makes it assured of acceptance. What I have done is yours, what I have to do is yours, being part in all I have, devoted yours. Were my worth greater, my duty would show greater; meantime, as it is, it is bound to your Lordship, to whom I wish long life still lengthened with all happiness."

The dedication is more relaxed; "The love I dedicate to your Lordship is without end"; and the poet is confident that it will be accepted. He asserts, "were my worth greater, my duty would show greater". The word "duty" has a special significance to Shakespeare. It is a positive word, as is clear from his plays. M. cbeth speaks of Duncan's part "to receive our duties", and our duties "Are to your throne and state children and servants" (I, iv, 23-24). In *As You Like It*, Adam, a part reputedly played by Shakespeare, says : "When service sweat for duty not for meed !" (II, iii, 56). This is presented in terms of the sacking of a city, while in *Titus Andronicus* the rape and mutilation of Lavinia and the subsequent familiar revenge is again related to the overthrow of civil order and justice, as Virgilian, Ovidian, and Senecan analogues are woven together to reinforce the Roman context of the play. During the Renaissance duty was an important concept, and it indicated "noble service". As expressed in sonnets 57 and 58, it is clear that it is an expression of an ideal service and a moving plea for patronage.

"Lucrece" is a very tense and sombre poem. The catalytic theme of rape seems to have inspired the poet to write a long poem. As a young poet of great promise, Shakespeare seems to let himself go and use as many digressions as possible. There is no limit to his poetical imagination. But the only disturbing incident is the seize of Troy, not really conducive to the theme, though a story of great attraction. It occupies about twenty-five stanzas, and Shakespeare's description of the fight is vivid, and realistic. However, the opening stanza states the theme of this story, based in Rome. It is "Of Collatine's fair love, Lucrece the chaste", ravished by "Lust-breathe'd Tarquin". The conflict is also stated:

> Within whose face beauty and virtue striv'd
> Which of them both should underprop her fame. (52-53)

Tarquin's treachery and lust are picturesquely described. Lust and murder are contrasted with the purity of the lamb.

> The silly lambs; pure thoughts are dead and still,
> While lust and murder wakes to stain and kill. (167-68)

He is poised between "desire and dread" and also conscious of his "loathsome enterprise". A debate whether to undertake the task of "naked armur of still slaughtered lust" (188) or "controls his thoughts unjust" (189) prepares the mind of the poet for the creation of tragic characters of immense tumult or of the disposition of "To be or not to be" in situations which demand action. The narrative is slow and repetitive but prepares the poet for his creations of tragic heroes with tumultuous feelings : Tarquin's criminal intent is clearly analysed : he is warned of "ambitious foul infirmity".

"Such hazard now must doting Tarquin make,/Pawning his honour to obtain his lust" (155-56). Such feelings of torment are seen in Shakespeare's tragic heroes and in Sonnet 129. There are echoes of *Macbeth*, with sound accompanying crime: "the Owl's shriek" and "the fatal bellman"; so are the noises of owls and wolves which are "death-boding cries" (165). Tarquin is not without conscience, which stabs him sharply. He is aware of selling himself to the devil, the eternal jewel given to the common enemy of man:

> What win I if I gain the thing I seek ?
> A dream, a breath, a froth of fleeting joy.
> Who buys a minute's mirth to wail a week ?
> Or sells eternity to get a toy ?
> For one sweet grape who will the vine destroy ?
> Or what found beggar, but to touch the crown,
> Would with the sceptre straight be strucken down? (211-17)

The situations are dramatically contrived, yet the characters are living; their make-up to be formed later, is demonstrated in the plays to come. Tarquin picks up Lucertia's gloves from the rushes, pricking her finger with the medal sticking out of it. Unmindful of these omens, he enters her chamber—a scene strongly reminiscent of that involving Iachimo and Imogen in *Cymbeline* :

> Her lily hand her rosy cheek lies under,
> Coz'ning the pillow of a lawful kiss. (386-87)

"Like a virtuous monument", Lucrece lies "To be admired of

lewd unhallowed eyes" (392). There are descriptions of various parts of her body, which correspond with those in *Kamasutra*: "Her breasts like marigolds" is a sensuous mage. But Tarquin, full of lust, is prepared "To kill thine honor with thy live's decay" (516). "Venus and Adonis" and "Rape of Lucrece" show the versatality of the dramatic poet in a bewilderingly rich creation of two different worlds.

NOTES

1. Biographia Literaria (1907), II. p. 19.
2. F.T. Prince, *The Poems*, Arden Shakespeare (London : Methuen, 1976), p. XXXVII.
3. *Ibid.*, Prince,
4. See *The Winter's Tale* IV, iv.
5. T.W. Baldwin argues that Shakespeare has taken pattern from Ovid's *Amors* 11, 6. See. "On the literary Genetics of *Shakespeare's Poems and Sonnets*," Alabama, Ill : University of Illinois Press, 1950, p. 363.
6. Prince, xxxix.

14

SONNETS

There is no comprehensive interpretation of Shakespeare's sonnets. Sidney Lee regarded them as "literary exercises"; Robert Gittings, in *Shakespeare's Rival* (1960), suggested that the "rival" poet was Gervase Markham—a poet who could not bear the description of "the proud full sail of his great verse". A.L. Rowse, in his biography of Shakespeare (1963), his edition of the sonnets (1964), and in his biography of Marlowe (1964) asserts that the rival poet was Marlowe and that the sonnets were addressed to Southampton (to whom, of course, Shakespeare dedicated "Venus and Adonis" and "Lucrece"). Rowse's publication of *The Poems of Shakespeare's Dark Lady Salve Deus Rex Judoerum* by Emilia Camer (1978) seems to affirm his claim without scholarly doubts. J. Dover Wilson disapproves of Rowse's theory (derived largely from Stopes) and claims that the sonnets were written to Shakespeare's other known patron, William Herbert, later Earl of Pembroke, and that the rival poet was George Chapman. Leslie Hotson, who agreed with Rowse that the rival poet was Marlowe, asserted that Mr. W.H.—"the onlie begetter of these insuing sonnets" was William Hatcliffe; his method is ingenious but unconvincing.

There is no single interpretation of acceptable theory of the characters that figure in the Sonnets. Mr. Wilt may be William Herbert, Earl of Pembroke : Sir William Harvey (Southampton's stepfather); William Hatcliffe; or (with the initials reversed) Henry Wriothesley, Earl of Southampton. The rival poet may be Marlowe or Chapman—though Marlowe, Raleigh's friend, is not likely to have been welcomed by Southampton, the associate of Essex. And Chapman is not known to have dedicated anything to either of Shakespeare's patrons until much later, and then only in terms which scarcely imply new encouragement. The Sonnets are delightful poetic trifles written on and off, which have some relation to the plays,—they are indeed "literary exrcises". Most of the critics assert their own arguments and refuse to see what others feel:

> Ah ! what a dusty answer gets the soul
> When hot for certainties!

Critics need not worry about three main characters in the Sonnets—recipient, rival poet, and dark lady. These are details for biographies; their study helps, however, in dating the plays. It is the concern of critics to decide whether the Sonnets in the 1609 edition were printed in the correct order.

Shakespeare seems to be "a rebel in the tradition of the Renaissance sonnet". The Sonnets are designed as groups of lyrics around particular themes of realism as opposed to the employment of allegory. The orthodox sonnet is normally Platonic, comparing the ideal with the real, while Shakespeare compares one reality with another. Traditionally, the sonnet compares ideal figure with symbolical reference of inference to a real one, whereas Shakespeare deliberately compares his friendship for a person with love between the sexes. Petrarch's sonnets deal with a Platonic ideal and a mortal woman; Shakespeare's concern the friendship between a highborn patron and humble poet and love between a man and dark lady. Petrarch's concern is earth and heaven, while Shakespeare's is earth alone. So Shakespeare, in a way, is an innovator in the tradition of British realism and prophetic of modern literature. Many have continued where Shakespeare left off.

The Sonnets, which are uneven in achievements, are close to "Venus and Adonis" in style as well as in theme. They are dated by alleged topical allusion, by reference to facts in the biographies of the supposed recipients, and by parallels with the plays. These methods have yielded controversial results. It is difficult to pin down topical allusions. Critics like Hotson feel that the line "The mortal moon hath her eclipse endured" refers to the destruction of the Spanish Armada, which sailed in crescent formation, while others feel that "the mortal moon" (107) refers to Queen Elizabeth. Between the defeat of the Spanish Armada in 1588, the Queen's death in 1603 there is a gap of fifteen years, and it therefore becomes difficult to date the Sonnets. This takes away our faith in biographical facts. A rewarding method is to see the sonnets in relation to the plyas, but their vivid imagery and description of love are forever charming.

Out of the one hundred and fifty-four Sonnets, the first one hundred and twenty-six are addressed to the patron-friend; then twenty-six are to a 'Dark Lady' and the last two deal with a myth about Cupid and contain references to the mineral springs at Bath. The last two are like an impersonal cadenza, witty and light, but disillusioned: "Love's fire heats water, water cools not love" (154), which is a kind of mood reminiscent of the ending of *Love's Labour's Lost*, where the comic ending is diminished by the sad news. Shakespeare, like all good poets of his own and succeeding ages, always had his mind on the finished poem as a work of art. His concern was not the romantic concern with self-expression but with composing a good sonnet, or a good song or a good pastoral. He kept in mind the audience for whom he wrote—a mistress, a learned and a witty friend, or a visitor reading an epigraph on a tombstone.

Although written at different times of the poet's imaginative life, there seems to be some arrangement or division among the Sonnets. The first comprises 1-126, which are addressed to the poet's young friend and patron, a person of high social status. Hence the poet assumes the role of an adviser. In the first sixteen sonnets (felicitously known as "the procreative sonnets") he appeals to a young man to marry and beget children and thus defeat mortality. These are derived partly from Erasmus' *De Scribendis Epistolie* and Sidney's *Arcadia*. Then there is a change, and Shakespeare speaks of the immortalising power of poetry and his own relationship with his friend—his jealousy of the rival poet, his relinquishment of his mistress, and his gradual realisation that his love is only partially returned. Many of the best sonnets are devoted to the celebration of the evil enchantments of the Dark Lady, and these are also concerned with the threat "to Time to beauty and love". Although he believed that his verse would immortalise his friend's youthful beauty, Shakespeare was aware (as Ulysses expressed it in *Troilus and Cressida*) that love and friendship were subjects 'envious and caluminating Time, says Kenneth Muir, commenting on Shakespeare's view on time and *The Metamorphoses* the last book of Ovid's on Pythagorean philosophy. Shakespeare complains of time's "injurious hand", "no stronger than a flower" is less enduring than lofty towers and the seas eternal, which are both slaves to Time, and that his friend will grow old and die:

> Ruin hath taught me thus to ruminate—
> That time will come and take my love away.

In this context of his lamentation for mutability, Sonnet 116 is a brilliant exposition. It also expresses the void which the death of Hammet (Shakespeare's only son) had left in his life:

> Let me not to the marriage of true minds
> Admit impediments. Love is not love
> Which alters when it alteration finds,
> Or bends with the remover to remove:
> O, no! it is an ever-fixed mark,
> That looks on tempests and is never shaken;
> It is the star to every wand' ring bark,
> Whose worth's unknown, although his height be taken
> Love's not Time's fool, though rosy lips and cheeks
> Within his bending sickle's compass come;
> Love alters not with his brief hours and weeks,
> But bears it out even to the edge of doom.
> If this be error, and upon me provd,
> I never writ, nor not man ever loved.

All beauty decays; it is within the compass of Time's scythe. But love seems to be above time : it endures "even to the edge of doom"—which may mean both doomsday and the death of the lover.

Through the rich imagery of poetic language, Shakespeare's personal life in literary, theatrical, and court circles constantly reveals itself in fascinating flashes. Sonnets are not constructed according to any prescription although T.W. Baldwin claims that they are, according to the prescription of the rhetorician the first quatrain being the *propositio*, the second a form of *ratio*, and the final couplet some from of conclusion or *complexio*. Some of the sonnets cannot be fit into the scheme. In No. 33 for exmple, the first quatrain describes a magnificant sunrise, the second describes the covering of the sun by clouds, the third applies this image to his friend's withdrawal of love, and the couplet announces the poet's own constancy. So also in No. 30, where the first quatrain describes the poet's sad memory, in which he summons up "remembrance of things past", the second gives examples of his sorrows, the third repeats the first, and the couplet ends thus : "All losses are restored and sorrows end".

One is interested in the sonnets as poems. In the best of them the lines and quatrains are bound together by sound as well as sense. Sonnet 71 is a very good example of the mingling of sound and sense:

No longer mourn for me when I am dead
Than you shall hear the surly sullen bell
Give warning to the world that I am fled
From this vile world, with vilest worms to dwell;
Nay, if you read this line, remember not
The hand that writ it; for I love you so,
That I in your sweet thoughts would be forgot,
If thinking on me then should make you woe.
O! if—I say, you look upon this verse,
When I perhaps compounded am with clay,
Do not so much as my poor name rehearse,
But let your love even with my life decay;
Lest the wise world should look into your moan,
And mock you with me after I am gone.

The phrases are linked by simple alliteration : "Mourn for me", "Warning to the world", "would...worry, "compounder . . . clay", "let my love even with my life", lest the wise world should look". But there is variation; as professor Muir notices, the linkage is reinforced by the alliteration of medial and terminal letters. For example, in the first line, the initial N is echoed in *longer*, mourn and when. In the second line the L of *longer*, is repeated four times.

"Then you shall hear the surly sullen bell"—and there are more l's in lines 3 and 4. All through the sonnet there is a predominance of m,n and L. This contributes to the effect of a lament and goes side by side with the extensive variety of vowel sounds. There are also other sonnets (such as No. 73) which are really complex in character. Thre equatrains of Sonnet 73 give parallel metaphorical statements on the poet's sense of growing old : "yellow leaves", "Bare ruin'd choirs". This sonnet tells us that the poet, who was thirty, was feeling the sense of growing old, as the lives of most Elizabethans were short. His friend is ten years younger, and Shakespeare feels the coming of old age. He compares his age to late autumn, to twilight, and to fading embers. But of this friend's love for him, he says it is brief, as it has not many years left:

> This thou perceive'st, which make thy love more strong.
> To love that well which thou must leave ere long.

In reading sonnets (100-25,) we notice a sobering tone. The poet boasts of fidelity at a time when the patron has fallen "under the blow of thralled discontent". The strong imagery adds to the sobering mood. In the final couplet to No.102, he says:

> Therefore, like her, I sometimes hold my tongue,
> Because I would not dull you with my song.

One finds a great deal of interest in the group celebrating the Dark Lady (127-52). There is harmony, charm, and wit in them. She must have been a great beauty (besides, being cultured) to lure one of the greatest poets of the period. In poems which abound in contradictions, the poet charmingly tells his friend of the woman's depravity and his unhappy infatuation; he wants to keep the woman for himself; if he does not succeed, he is prepared to surrender her favours. All this appears magnanimous for he can return to the patron: "These blenches gave my heart another youth".

Whatever may be the theme of the sonnets, behind them is a fine, richly imaginative poet. He is impressionable, mercurial, witty, melancholy—fretting under social oppression, but a king of imagination. The sonnets are a human document and deal with human problems—love, friendship, and sensual love. The 'I' of the sonnets is real; the poems abound in topical allusions and show certain parallels to situations in the plays. Most of the critics pay little attention to their literary qualities. They are little poems—rounded, neat, and taut. One can visualise a humble, jealous, devoted poet addressing the patron and also peep into the heart of the man addressing the opposite sex in all the ecstasy and bitterness, fancy and frivolity of love. The sonnets appeal to scholars as well as ordinary readers. While the scholars raise interrogatives of doubt of date and origin, the ordinary reader finds them "all compact".

15

CONCLUSION

Comedy, especially Shakespeare's, is didactic in outlook. It was meant to mingle moral instruction with delight in the work of the playwright. The comic art is bewilderingly rich in its techniques, situations, and characters. In classical India, too, it was the most enchanting form, and *Kavyeshu natakam ramyam*, But in both comedy and tragedy the poets and artists penetrate the depth of human nature. Since the Greek plays of the fifth century B.C. the playwright has acted as artist-teacher, the play having an end outside itself: the design of the classical and Elizabethan comedies was to lead the public into a way of virtue. However, comedy by its very nature is a much more ephemeral thing and much more closely bound to its own day and age than tragedy, and it normally follows the language of the day. But the pleasure of comedy lives longer than the pain of tragedy, though the comic world is not the escapist, glamorous world of imagination but a very serious world of problems.

Shakespeare borrowed from Plautus and Terence, yet the tenor of his plays is very different from his originals. Like the comedies of classical times, they are written with a purpose but wrapped up in a bit of romance. Not that Shakespeare is falling between the two stools (the classical comedy and the romantic farce), for he gives the borrowed material some sort of solidity and originality. The Indian classical playwrights depended on the epics (the *Ramayana* and the *Mahabharata* and other stories of Buddhism and Jainism) and consequently a classical comedy sometimes is loaded with philosophical doctrines. Sometimes, too, it is a weak evasion of reality, as in *Mrichakataka*. But Shakespeare takes great care to balance the religious and the secular. In him the religious outlook of the East and the secular outlook of the West seem to exist side by side. The age of Shakespeare witnessed the birth of a new spirit in every sphere of human activity, and this new spirit, known as the Renaissance, expressed itself in its unusually rich variety in the plays of Shakespeare and his contemporaries, notably in comedies that are as serious as tragedies in their make-up and that embody the new view of man and woman. Sanskrit plays and Shakespeare express the values of life with extraordinary eloquence and force.

It will be seen from this brief survey of the early comedies of Shakespeare that he was influenced by the theory that comedy should be didactic, and that his plays are close to the spirit of Roman comedies and the classical plays of India. The tenor of the narrative poems and Sonnets is close to these early comedies.

In the prologue to Bhavabhuti's melodramatic play, *Malati and Madhva*, he writes as though he has endured a career harassed by conflicts. He tells the public: "How little do they know who speak of us with censure. The entertainment is not for them. Possibly some one exists, or will exist, of similar tastes with myself, for time is boundless, and the world is wide". This could as well have been said by Shakespeare. Let us accept Bhavabhuti's invitation to study the minds that are a very treasure of opals.

INDEX